FORGOTTEN SCRIPTS

FORGOTTEN SCRIPTS

Their Ongoing Discovery and Decipherment

CYRUS H. GORDON

REVISED AND ENLARGED EDITION

BASIC BOOKS, INC., PUBLISHERS
New York

Library of Congress Cataloging in Publication Data

Gordon, Cyrus Herzl, 1908–
  Forgotten scripts.

  Bibliography: p. 210
  Includes index.
  1. Extinct languages. 2. Inscriptions—History.
3. Writing—History. I. Title.
P901.G65 1982 C.2 417'.7'093   81–68822
ISBN 0–465–02484–X   AACR2

Dedicated to
David Rose
for his enlightened support of
Ebla Studies

CONTENTS

FOREWORD TO
THE REVISED
AND ENLARGED
EDITION

There is no dearth of books bearing on forgotten scripts and their decipherment.[1] Adding one more is warranted only if it offers something distinctive.

Very few of the published volumes are based on a firsthand control of virtually all of the primary sources. The knowledge explosion has brought on an age of high specialization that makes the mastery of all the main forgotten scripts well-nigh impossible for our younger scholars.

1. For examples, see I. J. Gelb, *A Study of Writing*, rev. ed. (Chicago: University of Chicago Press, 1963); F. J. W. Barber, *Archaeological Decipherment: A Handbook* (Princeton: Princeton University Press, 1974); Maurice Pope, *The Story of Decipherment: From Egyptian Hieroglyphic to Linear B*, with 118 illustrations and a map (London: Thames & Hudson Ltd., 1975); and G. R. Driver, *Semantic Writing: From Pictograph to Alphabet*, new rev. ed. (London: Oxford University Press, 1976). All these books have useful charts of various scripts.

But even among the senior citizens of academia it is exceedingly hard to find anyone well versed in both cuneiform
and Egyptian. Since those two fields remain the corner-
stones of our topic, the limitation is serious.

There is another basic factor missing in current books on
the subject. The authors have not personally gone through
the various stages of the process: excavating the inscriptions, copying the texts, mastering the languages, and so
forth, down to scoring the actual breakthrough. I hope that
the reader will be inducted into the world of the pioneers,
a world fraught with brief ecstasies and prolonged frustrations.

Pioneers open fields and leave the refining process to less
inspired but more meticulous successors. I shall endeavor
to render justice to the refining process, but my sympathies
are squarely with the pioneers, and against their destructive critics.

Criticizing pioneering work often goes hand in hand
with trying to impose an unrealistic standard of perfectionism on those who blaze new trails in an uncharted terrain.
My own teacher, Roland G. Kent, was a master of Classics
and Indo-European linguistics. His book on Old Persian
remains standard. While he knew full well that Georg
Grotefend had made the first crucial steps in deciphering
Old Persian, Kent's pedantic spirit impelled him to brand
all of Grotefend's other readings as sorry stuff. We need
both kinds of scholar: the Grotefends for opening new
vistas, and the Kents for refining them into scientific disciplines. Few and far between are those who can function at
both levels.

The pioneers and the refiners have different methods of
procedure. For example, the pioneer often resorts to the
etymological method. Thus, a bronze adze from Ugarit

bears the inscriptions *rb khnm*. The early pioneers found *rb* meaning "chief" and *khnm* meaning "priests" in the Hebrew dictionaries. This indeed gives the correct translation; the adze belonged to the High Priest (literally, the "chief of the priests"). But as Ugaritology became more developed, dependence on the etymological method alone became passé. In a passage, *mlak zbl ym // t'dt tpt nhr*,[2] the word *t'dt* is defined as "testimonies" in the Hebrew lexica. The etymological method would indicate that Ugaritic *t'dt* was impersonal and abstract. Yet the context does not permit us to translate it as "the messengers of Prince Sea // the testimonies of Judge River." The contextual method must now be employed. The context tells us that *t'dt* is a synonym of the parallel word "messengers." Accordingly we translate it "the messengers of Prince Sea // the emissaries of Judge River." A critic in the 1980s should not forget that while the etymological method of the pioneers is no longer adequate for determining the meaning of Ugaritic vocabulary, it was the principal source of defining Ugaritic vocabulary that opened up the interpretation of the texts in the 1930s. What is rightly looked at askance in the 1980s was a necessary and productive method half a century earlier.

There is also a compelling reason for updating this book at this time. A major discovery has come to light since the first edition of *Forgotten Scripts* in 1968. The extensive archives of Ebla[3] are of importance not only because they

2. The main principle of ancient Near Eastern poetry is parallelism, whereby one utterance is balanced by another of related meaning and bulk. The two slashes are a conventional way among modern scholars to indicate the division between parallel members. The lack of vowels in the transliteration will be explained, and repeatedly illustrated, in the following chapters on the decipherments.

3. Among the first books written to introduce Ebla to the general public, the first to appear in English is Chaim Bermant and Michael Weitzman, *Ebla: A Revelation in Archaeology* (New York: Times Books, 1979). For the archaeology, see

provide us with the materials for reconstructing the hitherto unknown Eblaite language, but also because they affect our understanding of other scripts, languages, literatures, and histories of various Near East and Mediterranean regions. The Early Bronze Age date of the Ebla library gives us more depth in answering old questions and asking new ones.

Our subject is not static. Because the forgotten scripts are growing through fresh major finds, they are ongoing and dynamic. The reader should get a sense not only of the accomplishments in the past but also of this ongoing process. Adventure of the mind can be a permanent way of life; it need not be a dead-end road. Only when we feel that we have gone far enough along the way, have we reached the dead end. We have no control over chronological age, but no particular birthday obliges us to stop learning and seeking. Two thousand years ago a sage taught, "It is not for thee to finish the task, but neither art thou free to desist therefrom."[4]

While the decipherments in themselves are triumphs of Western civilization, their significance lies primarily in the value of the literatures they have opened up. Chapter 9 has been added to provide "a sampling of unlocked treasures" to convey to the reader an impression of the variety and quality of the erstwhile mute texts that can now speak.

This book obviously does not aim at exhausting the reader by attempting to cover every detail. To the contrary, it is an invitation to delve more deeply into those aspects of the subject that most interest the reader. Humanistic

---

the volume by the excavator, Paolo Matthiae, *Ebla: An Empire Rediscovered* (Garden City, N.Y.: Doubleday, 1981). For the tablets, see Giovanni Pettinato, *The Archives of Ebla* (Garden City, N.Y.: Doubleday, 1981).

4. An aphorism of Rabbi Ṭarfon in the *Mishna, Ethics of the Fathers* 2:21.

scholarship, though not lucrative, is a rewarding way of life. As a teacher through this book I hope to lead some gifted young students into that life.[5]

Cyrus H. Gordon

January 1982

---

5. I thank my student Mr. Gary Speziale for his handsome drawings of the Egyptian hieroglyphs appearing in this book.

The illustrations in chapter 7 are reproduced from my book *Evidence for the Minoan Language* with the kind permission of Ventnor Publishers Inc.

I am especially grateful to Mr. Allan R. Bomhard for permitting me to use his personally prepared, camera-ready copy of my article on Minoan as the basis for my treatment of the subject in chapter 7. His camera-ready copy of my article will appear in *Bono Homini Donum: Essays in Historical Linguistics in Memory of J. Alexander Kerns,* edited by Y. Arbeitman and A. R. Bomhard (Amsterdam: John Benjamins, 1981).

PREFACE TO
THE FIRST
EDITION

The nineteenth and twentieth centuries have been ages of scientific progress beyond the dreams of man in earlier periods. Sumero-Akkadian mythology tells us of a hero, Etana, who flew heavenward on the back of an eagle, and Greek mythology relates how Daedalus made wings so that he and his son Icarus could fly through the air; but what pre-modern man ever conceived of the spacecraft now circling the earth and other planets or reaching the moon, with ever greater achievements unfolding in rapid succession? Nor are the miracles in other branches of modern science less remarkable. What is less well known is that there are comparably great achievements in the humanities that started in the nineteenth century and are continuing with unabated progress today.

With the passing of antiquity in Roman times, Western

civilization came to be conceived as starting with the three classical forms of Mediterranean culture—Israel, Greece, and Rome. Homer and the Bible stood at the beginning of recorded history, and everything earlier was regarded as prehistoric. And yet a succession of travelers and curious intellectuals knew that in Egypt and Iran there were monuments and inscriptions of a distant past. Less spectacular to the visitor's eye were the ruined cities of Mesopotamia, but they were nonetheless associated with cuneiform texts that concealed an ancient story. Hebrew, Greek, and Latin literature preserved enough collateral information to provide the future decipherers with the necessary background. All that was needed were the men with the dream, the dedication, the knowledge, the mind, and the courage to persevere in the search for truth.

We are about to tell the story of how forgotten scripts were deciphered and lost languages recovered, thus adding two thousand years to the documented span of Western civilization. Greece and Israel no longer stand at the dawn of history. Thanks to the decipherment of Egyptian and cuneiform, there are now fifteen centuries of recorded history in the cradle of Western culture, before the Greeks and the Hebrews appeared on the scene. Moreover, the earliest inscriptions pertaining to the Hellenes and Israelites antedate the composition of the *Iliad* and of Genesis.

The desire to solve the mystery of esoteric inscriptions is almost as old as writing itself. The most familiar legend of decipherment appears in the Book of Daniel: once upon a time Belshazzar of Babylon was confronted with a mysterious message wondrously inscribed by a disembodied hand upon his palace wall. None of the sages could decipher it except Daniel, who by divine inspiration read the Aramaic text *mene mene tekel upharsin* and without hesitation interpreted it flawlessly.[1] The modern decipherer, like Daniel, needs inspiration, but unlike Daniel he also requires a background in philology and history. Technologically the decipherers of cuneiform and hieroglyphic texts resemble Daniel somewhat as the Wright brothers resemble Etana and Daedalus.

The decipherments of the forgotten scripts in the cradles of Western culture have not only revealed millennia of history; they have also opened a Pandora's box of problems that may prove to be more difficult to solve than the decipherments. While Darwinism was hitting at what eighteenth-century rationalism had left of traditional religion, the cuneiform texts revealed a pagan mythology that was used as ammunition to blow up the vestiges of biblical faith. If Noah's Flood was only a late Hebrew copy of the ancient Babylonian Deluge, what could one still accept in sacred Scripture? The net result was a tendency to split the public into two opposing camps: atheists and obscurantists. The one maintained that science and archaeological discovery exposed religious tradition as fallacy and fraud. The other rejected as pernicious the testimony of science and the newly deciphered texts. We are still suffering from this needless dichotomy, which has bred a lost generation seeking meaning in history and life.

The illogical crisis came in the Scopes trial, with two remarkable men—the atheist Clarence Darrow and the "defender of the faith" William Jennings Bryan—championing the opposing viewpoints. It was not necessary then, as it is not necessary now, to reject either scientific

---

1. Daniel 5, where the interest in the text is to interpret a prophecy that would otherwise remain secret. Today our interest in inscriptions is rather for the information they provide on the past. Somewhat similarly, the ancients interpreted dreams as announcements of, or advice on, things to come, whereas we interpret dreams as reflexes of past experience.

enlightenment or our traditional heritage. To be civilized and complete, we must accept scientific enlightenment and our traditional heritage, each in its proper place. Neglect of either is disastrous. Science without tradition can produce technicians but not cultured men; tradition without science can breed learned but not rational men.

The succession of decipherers whose work has revolutionized the humanities was the product of an intellectual atmosphere that we may trace to the Renaissance. That rebirth embodied an interest in the ancient past. Although it stressed the classical heritage of Greece and Rome, the preoccupation of artists and scholars with Scripture kept the Bible lands in the picture. Moreover, there was a growing curiosity about the world as a whole, culminating in the Age of Discovery. The voyages of Columbus, Magellan, and other pioneers sailing the seven seas and exploring distant shores were not merely the results of improved technical capabilities; they were also the product of the enlarged frame of mind in Western Europe, ushered in by the Renaissance.

The immediate prologue of the Age of the Decipherments is the Enlightenment of the eighteenth century. The excavation of Herculaneum and Pompeii then raised the interest in archaeology and ancient texts to new heights.[2] Intellectual curiosity had added Oriental studies to the university repertoire. Travelers like Carsten Niebuhr (1733–1815) visited the cradles of Western civilization and brought back and published facsimiles of inscriptions in forgotten scripts. The interest in faraway places peers through the

---

2. For readable introductions to the subject, see Leo Deuel, *Testaments of Time* (New York: Alfred A. Knopf, 1965), pp. 55–77, and C. W. Ceram, *Hands on the Past* (New York: Alfred A. Knopf, 1966), pp. 61–68 (selected from the writings of J. J. Winkelmann and A. Goldsmidt).

literature of the times. Samuel Johnson's *Rasselas* is set in Abyssinia. Voltaire's satirical stories unfold in distant lands, ranging from Babylon to the New World. A constellation of interests and activities was pointing toward the decipherments of the nineteenth century. Archaeology, in the form of both exploration and excavation, was under way. Texts as well as monuments were reaching Europe from the lands of the forgotten scripts. Arabic, Syriac, Coptic, Ethiopic, and other Near Eastern languages were being increasingly added to the old repertoire of Hebrew, Greek, and Latin. European involvement in India had led to the study of Sanskrit and the ancient Persian texts of the Parsees.

At the close of the eighteenth century, Napoleon, with an eye on far-off India, embarked on the invasion of Egypt to open a new era. He catapulted the Near East into its modern period, which is characterized by Western European influence. He also initiated the age of large-scale collecting, studying, and publishing of nonclassical inscriptions, art, and architecture. Specifically, he ushered in the Age of Egyptology.

While Napoleon's invasion of Egypt was more spectacular than events in western Iran, where the Achaemenian kings had left their inscriptions, the cuneiform materials had been discovered and some of the men destined to decipher them had been born during the last third of the eighteenth century.

The open-mindedness and intellectual curiosity of that age were, as always, too much for reactionary men. Both fundamentalisms—secular and religious—gained in momentum when confronted with new developments. Secular fundamentalism stemmed largely from classicists who objected to giving credit to the "barbaric" civilizations such as the Egyptians or the Phoenicians. Religious fundamentalism is opposed to connections between the Chosen People and their heathen neighbors. Both fundamentalisms are essentially the same, prompted as they are by the desire to keep an ideal free of outside contamination. Classical fundamentalism was unleashed after Champollion's decipherment of Egyptian. Religious fundamentalism broke loose with renewed vigor after the announcement of the biblical parallels in cuneiform literature.

The intellectual life of the West took a strange turn by the end of the nineteenth century. Hitherto, fully educated men had tried to reckon with Hebrew, Greek, and Latin as their threefold heritage. In the poems of Milton we see the blending at every turn. For a long time after Harvard University was founded in the seventeenth century, the valedictorian address was delivered in Hebrew. The Yale emblem still carries its Hebrew as well as Latin text. But with the growth of knowledge in the nineteenth century, specialization had begun to separate Classics from Hebrew. The intellectuals reared in the classical tradition were committed to the uniqueness of the Greek and Roman ideal, but at the same time, as long as they professed to be Christians, they were forced to reckon with the divine inspiration of the Bible. How were they to cling to a twofold ideal, which they themselves held to be in opposition? Artificial barriers were accordingly erected as people reasoned somewhat as follows: "The Hebrew was a genius in religion and morality even as the Greek was a genius in philosophy and science. The one was spiritual and Oriental; the other was rational and European."

The net result was that instead of being Mediterranean peoples flourishing during the same centuries, Greeks and Hebrews were so separated by a contrived chasm that they might just as well have been from opposite poles, if not from different planets. This led to a kind of truce: since two different groups of scholars foster Classics and Old Testament studies respectively, each is to help preserve the peace by staying in his own terrain. The old-fashioned classicist does not as a rule welcome any evidence of profound Phoenician impact on Greece, and the well-adjusted Hebrew scholar is quite content to shut his eyes to Mycenaean and Minoan developments even though he knows that Palestine is named after an Aegean people called the Philistines.[3]

Thus, the Enlightenment of the eighteenth century has left us a twofold legacy—the expanding mentality that produced the decipherments and the reaction that not only prescribes blinkers but resists the mounting evidence of mutual relationships and a common heritage in the ancient Mediterranean.

CYRUS H. GORDON

March 1968

---

3. Since the above was written in 1968, more and more classicists on the one hand, and biblical scholars on the other, are shaking off secular and religious parochialism. The old guard has not so much been converted as replaced by a new generation raised in an ecumenical age and exposed to new sources and fresh approaches.

FORGOTTEN SCRIPTS

1

CODES AND
CIPHERS

There is a professional world of codes and ciphers that has evolved an elaborate science and technology of its own. Every government and many private agencies use secret writing for their classified communications. There are differences between solving forgotten scripts and modern cryptography. Forgotten scripts were not written to defy interpretation to all but the writer and the receiver; they were meant to be intelligible to the entire literate public. The methods employed in solving enemy systems of cryptography, however, are of great value to the decipherer of ancient scripts, and it is not surprising that since the First World War some of the successful decipherments have been made by scholars who have had experience in military cryptanalysis. Accordingly, a survey of the elements of cryptography will help us understand the decipherment of the ancient systems.

Codes and ciphers are two different forms of cryptography. Codes deal with the substitution of whole words or even phrases. By merely taking a dictionary and writing in a code number next to each word, we can transform the dictionary into a code book. For example if the dictionary lists more than 9,999 words but not more than 99,999, a five-digit code is indicated. If the dictionary starts: *a, aback, abacus, abandon, abandoned, abase, abashed, abate, abbess, abbey, abbot, abbreviate, abbreviation, abdicate,* . . . we can assign the following code numbers:

a	00001	abate	00008
aback	00002	abbess	00009
abacus	00003	abbey	00010
abandon	00004	abbot	00011
abandoned	00005	abbreviate	00012
abase	00006	abbreviation	00013
abashed	00007	abdicate	00014

The same book can be used for encoding and decoding messages because the sequence of the numbers follows the alphabetized words. This is therefore called a one-part code. Inherently, it is not good for secrecy, because as soon as the code breakers realize its nature, they can interpolate values. Thus, when they discover that 00001 is "a," they immediately have reason to believe that they are faced with a one-part code. If they solve any two code numbers (for example, 00004 = "abandon" and 00014 = "abdicate"), they know that an intermediate number comes between the two in the dictionary (00008 comes after "abandon" but before "abdicate").

A two-part code requires two different books: one in dictionary order for encoding and one with the code numbers in numerical order for decoding. Our encoding book could begin thus:

a	66789
aback	12834
abacus	92386
abandon	00004

Here there is no relation between the order of the code numbers and the alphabetized dictionary. The decoding book might begin thus:

00001	country
00002	fifteen
00003	debate
00004	abandon
00005	zebra
00006	escalate

The two-part code is a more secure system, but the preparation and distribution of the extra code books cost time and money. It pays to employ them only if they are used for reasonably long periods. Any code that is used extensively is vulnerable, however, because it is a law of secret writing that if the enemy intercepts enough of it, he can solve the system and reconstruct the code book through statistics and analysis. For in any language, the frequency and position of certain words provide the code breaker with ways of transforming coded messages into plain text.

Something else that makes codes vulnerable is spies and agents who steal, buy, or photocopy code books.

We might note also that codes (particularly commercial codes) are sometimes designed not for secrecy but to save on cablegram expenses. If "05638" means "Sell immediately the stock mentioned in your letter that we have just received," the cable or telegram will cost less than the full plain-text message. When we write the French abbreviation "R.S.V.P." after an invitation, we are doing something similar; it is a short way of saying, "Please tell us whether you will attend."

For maintaining secrecy, ciphers are generally used. Either the plain text or a coded message can be enciphered. Let us say that the following message is encoded in accordance with a two-part system thus:[1]

Plain text:	ENEMY PLANS ATTACK AT-DAWN			
Encoded text:	0931	5723	6288	9482

There is no reason to be sure that the enemy does not possess our code books, which have been in use for a long time. Accordingly, our cryptographic security staff has decided to protect our communications by agreeing, for example, to add 15 to the first group, 162 to the second, 1903 to the third, and then begin all over again (adding first 15, then 162, and finally 1903, and so forth).

Coded message:	0931	5723	6288	9482
Encipherment:	+ 15	+162	+1903	+15
Cryptogram:	0946	5885	8191	9497

The receiver gives the cryptogram to his cryptographer, who first deciphers it (by subtracting the encipherment) and then decodes the deciphered message into plain text.

The above type of encipherment is called an "additive."

1. Since a code book for simple messages in the field need not have more than 9,999 words or phrases, four-digit groups will suffice.

It can, of course, be applied directly to the plain text. Suppose our encipherment is 1-2-3; that is, we shall add 1 to the first letter, 2 to the second letter, and 3 to the third letter, and then begin over again (adding 1 to the fourth letter, 2 to the fifth letter, and 3 to the sixth, and so forth).

Plain text:	ENEMY PLANS ATTACK AT DAWN
Encipherment:	1 2 3 1 2 3 1 2 3 1 2 3 1 2 3 1 2 3 1 2 3 1
Cryptogram:	FPHNA SMCQT CWUCFL CW ECZO

When we add 1 to *e*, we go to the next letter in the alphabet *f*; when we add 2 to *n*, we go on to the second letter thereafter *p*; 3 added to *e* means the third letter thereafter is *h*.

Another kind of encipherment is transposition. For instance, we can interchange the positions of the letters in every pair of letters:

Plain text:	E N E M Y P L A N S A T T A C K A T D A W N
Cryptogram:	N E M E P Y A L S N T A A T K C T A A D N W

Here the cryptographer who deciphers the message will have to divide the plain text into words after transposing the cryptogram into plain text.

The simplest kind of encipherment is mono-alphabetic substitution. This means that each letter is always replaced by another definite letter:

Plain alphabet:	A B C D E F G H I J K L M N O P Q R S T U V W X Y Z
Cipher alphabet:	Z X C V B N M A S D F G H J K L P O I U Y T R E W Q

Taking the same plain text, we have:

ENEMY PLANS ATTACK AT DAWN

The cryptogram is now:

BJBHW LGZJI ZUUZCF ZU VZRJ

The cryptographer charged with deciphering this message will use the following chart (in which the cipher is alphabetized while the plain values now seem randomized):

Cipher alphabet: A B C D E F G H I J K L M N O P Q R S T U V W X Y Z
Plain alphabet: H E C J X K L M S N O P G F R Q Z W I V T D Y B U A

Mono-alphabetic substitution is easy to solve because in any known language the letters have known frequencies. A couple of pages enciphered by this method can be solved without any difficulty, provided the language is known. Shorter cryptograms are harder to solve because, without volume, statistics are not reliable. We shall take an example of mono-alphabetic substitution in order to illustrate what methods can be used in addition to statistics. The following cryptogram is to be deciphered into plain English:

VHBSJU XBT BDDJEFOUBMMZ EJTDPWFSFE CZ
B QFBTBOU JO OJOFUFFO IVOESFE BOE
UXFOUZFJHIU IF QMPXFE JOUP B NZDFOBFBO
UPNC BOE VOXJUUJOHMZ PQFOFE VQ B
OFX FSB PG EJTDPWFSZ

A frequency count tells us each letter is used so many times:

A B C D E F G H I J K L M
0 14 2 5 10 19 1 3 3 10 0 0 4

N O P Q R S T U V W X Y Z
2 17 7 4 0 5 4 11 4 2 5 0 6

It will be noted that some letters are of high frequency, others are of low frequency; the rest are in between. If we had a long cryptogram, we could solve the problem statistically without more ado. But in so short a text, statistics are not reliable. We note, however, that the letters of highest frequency are F and O (F, 19 times; and O, 17). One of these should be the letter *e*, which occurs more often than any other letter in English. We may expect the definite article "the" to occur in any English utterance, even if it be limited to a few lines. The three-letter words in the cryptogram are XBT, BOE (which occurs twice), OFX, and FSB. Disappointingly, none of these ends in F or O, and we conclude that, against all expectation, "the" does not appear in our message.

There is a one-letter word (B) that occurs three times, and it is a letter of great frequency. Now there are only two common words that we need to consider (for "O" is hardly used nowadays): "a" and "I." This letter happens to begin the three-letter word BOE, which occurs twice. There are many three-letter words beginning with *a* in English, but none is more common than "and." If BOE = "and," we have B = *a*, O = *n* and E = *d*. We shall apply these values and see if they yield good or bad readings elsewhere in the cryptogram. It will be noted that four words end in FE:

EJTDPWFSFE
IVOESFE
QMPXFE
PQFOFE

Since F is of the highest frequency (occurring 19 times) and we ruled out O = *e*, F should be *e*, giving us the suffix FE = *-ed* to indicate the past tense of verbs. Since the two-letter word JO ends with *n*, the first letter must be a vowel, and *a* is ruled out because B = *a*. This leaves *i* and *o* as the only possibilities since "an," "in," and "on" are the only two-letter English words ending in *n*. Now, in OJO-FUFFO, J = *o* would yield *noneUeen*, which is meaningless in English whatever value we ascribe to U; however, J = *i* allows us to take *nineUeen* as the only possible word in English—"nineteen"—showing that U = *t*. From this point on, the rest is easy. JOUP = *int-* can only be "into" with P = *o*. PQFOFE = *oQened* must be "opened" with Q = *p*. VQ = *Vp* can only be "up" with V = *u*. QFBTBOU = *peaTant* must be "peasant" with T = *s*. The skeleton of the number "nineteen IuOdSed and tXentZei-HIt" would not puzzle any cryptanalyst very long. It can be only "nineteen hundred and twenty-eight," which yields I = *h*, O = *n*, S = *r*, X = *w*, Z = *y*, and H = *g*. With these values, we can decipher our cryptogram to this extent:

```
VHBSJU XBT BDDJEFOUBMMZ EJTDPWFSFE CZ B
u   ar it was a    iden t a    y dis o  ered y a
QFBTBOU JO OJOFUFFO IVOESFE BOE
pe as an t  in nine te en hun dre d and
UXFOUZFJHIU IF QMPXFE JOUP B NZDFOBFBO
twent y ei ght he p  owed in to a   y en ae an
UPNC BOE VOXJUUJOHMZ PQFOFE VQ B OFX
to   and u nwi t t in    y o pe ned up a new
FSB PG EJTDPWFSZ
era o   dis o   ery
```

From this point the reader should be able to solve the rest. The plain text is given at the end of the chapter so that he may check his solution.

The world of cryptography is now quite complex. Encipherments that go in a cycle of three are easy to break because sooner or later the same words will reappear at the same point in the cycle, and once the cyclicity is solved, all the cryptanalyst needs is enough volume of intercepts to crack the system. Even a cycle of a hundred is not enough to protect a system that is used extensively. Security now may be sought by cycles that do not repeat until the million mark is passed. This can be done through complex machines; the sender and receiver have the same adjustable machines. The receiver must also know how to set his cryptographic machine to remove the encipherment. Such systems are difficult, if not impossible, to break by cryptanalysis. Espionage or some other kind of skulduggery can be more effective. Fortunately for our purposes, we do not have to delve into the highly complex mechanical and electronic methods of encipherment and decipherment. The ancient scripts that had to be deciphered were not secret systems devised to defy reading. They were made to be read and understood. The methods used to decode and decipher help us unravel the reading and translation of forgotten scripts and languages, but nothing that has come down to us from antiquity was enciphered by an electronic randomizer so that we require a complex device for unscrambling ancient cryptograms.

We must now differentiate the cryptographer from the cryptanalyst. The cryptographer uses the code books and cipher systems of his office. He does not handle enemy messages that require solution without benefit of code books and cipher keys. The cryptanalyst, on the other hand, deals precisely with messages that he must solve through analysis without code books and cipher keys. It is his business to decipher enemy cryptograms even if he has to break systems and reconstruct code books in the process. Our subject deals with decipherers whose role is like the cryptanalyst's rather than the cryptographer's.

Sometimes ancient texts are equipped with word dividers, which makes the task easier. But if the word dividers are not supplied, the decipherer has to edit his text and, by studying the repetitions, break up the text into its component words. For instance, if the preceding sentence were run together, a study of it would reveal that the sequence *the* occurs no less than four times and should therefore be some common word. If there is enough text, the words can be isolated even though they are run together. In Akkadian —one of the best known of the deciphered languages— words are not separated.

Collateral information is of prime importance in starting a decipherment as well as in interpreting a text even after the opening wedge has been made. If an enciphered message from Tehran is intercepted on a certain date, it may be assumed that it is written in Persian and deals with something that belongs to our world as revealed in the *New York Times* or the Tehran newspapers of that date. If a long cryptogram was sent from Paris to every French embassy at about the time Mitterrand took some major step or made some notable pronouncement, two assumptions can be made: (1) that the cryptogram is in French, and (2) that it deals with the news item from Paris that has just made the headlines. It has happened that codes and ciphers have been compromised by careless cryptographic clerks who have encoded and enciphered long dispatches whose plain texts have been published in the press. One of the rules of security in such cases is always to paraphrase and transpose the original before sending it as a cryptogram. Careless clerks are God's gift to the cryptanalyst charged with breaking foreign systems.[2]

2. One of the commonest faux pas made by cryptographic clerks is to insert proper names in plain text. This gives the enemy the opening wedge for deciphering the cryptogram by providing him with a clue to the context. It is interesting to note that proper names are among the most frequent keys in the decipherment of ancient scripts.

The problem that confronts the decipherer of ancient texts is that even if he correctly guesses what language they are in, he has no *New York Times* to tell him what the writers may have had on their minds when they composed the inscriptions. The collateral information may, however, be supplied from history. Herodotus's genealogical facts concerning the Achaemenian kings supplied the decipherers with the data they needed for cracking the cuneiform inscriptions of Persia and Mesopotamia. A knowledge of place names is also important. That "Knossos" should be found in the Linear B texts (see p. 128) from Knossos but not from Pylos and that "Pylos" should be found in the Linear B texts from Pylos but not from Knossos were correct assumptions that helped crack Linear B.

Not only are the names of kings and places important, but any knowledge one has of what was on the ancient scribe's mind and how he would be likely to express it can also help in deciphering ancient texts. There is a huge mass of ancient Near Eastern inscriptions that provide us with collateral information. By drawing on his knowledge of the language and of the collateral information, the decipherer can make inferences which may turn out to be right because they fit into some pattern inherent in the text. In a group of words that looked like cardinal numerals, the decipherers of Ugaritic rightly decided that the one with the pattern XYX had to be *tlt*, "three." None of the other cardinal numbers in Northwest Semitic fits this pattern.

Guesses of this kind are necessary, but they cannot be off the top of one's head; to be successful, they must reckon with the realities, or at least the probabilities, of the text to be deciphered. Even then most guesses are wrong, so that a prime quality in the cryptanalyst or decipherer is flexibility. Wrong guesses are usually exposed as incorrect by the fact that they lead to impossible combinations when applied elsewhere in the texts to be deciphered. But it is also necessary to follow through with the truth if a successful decipherment is to be achieved. Both Arthur Evans and Arthur Cowley individually got correct Greek values for Mycenaean words but they were not in a frame of mind to follow through. Evans had committed himself to a false premise (that the language was not Greek) and could not extricate himself. Without flexibility, decipherment is impossible. Guesses must be made, and it is the lucky guess that pays off. But for every lucky guess, hundreds of wrong ones must be scrapped.

Lucky guesses often take the form of the "probable word." Some three-letter combination in texts from Canaan ought to be b^cl "Baal" (the well-known Canaanite god). Hans Bauer, having determined the b and the l, spotted bXl as "Baal" and obtained the correct c value for X. His guess of the probable word turned out to be right, for $X = {}^c$ makes sense in all the other combinations.

We now must define what we mean by a "decipherment." Strictly speaking, the term applies to obtaining from scratch the pronunciation of the symbols in texts that cannot even be pronounced before the decipherment. Examples of this are afforded by the decipherment of Egyptian hieroglyphs, Old Persian cuneiform, the Cypriot syllabary, and the Ugaritic cuneiform alphabet. Decipherment does not imply that the language turns out to be new. The Cypriot texts turned out to be Greek; the Ugaritic language is close to Hebrew. The decipherment in both cases was successful because the language was known. The basic achievement of the decipherers was to determine the pronunciation of the symbols.

A different sort of accomplishment is the working out of a new language written in a known script. Sumerian did not have to be deciphered in the sense that Akkadian did; Sumerian is written in the same script, and Akkadian was worked out first. Since Akkadian belongs to the well-established Semitic family of languages, it has been recovered with a high degree of finesse, so that scholars are in agreement as to how any but the most problematic texts are to be translated. This is still not so with Sumerian, where the handful of top authorities do not always agree in translating many passages in the most familiar literary texts, such as Gudea's Cylinders, that have been known for nearly a century and republished many times.

In most essentials, of course, there is agreement in translating Sumerian texts, and the language whose very existence was unsuspected when Henry Rawlinson began his work is now richly documented. Sumerology fills libraries with tomes of autographed texts, translations, linguistic studies, and historical works. It has therefore been "deciphered," but no one person can be credited with its decipherment. The phonetic values of Sumerian signs came out of the decipherment and study of Akkadian; countless lexical and other school texts, including bilinguals, prepared in antiquity provide the firm basis for working out the vocabulary and grammar of Sumerian. And even so, with such an abundance of materials, it is taking a long time to refine Sumerology to a point where it can be reduced to clear rules with the modicum of agreement among the experts necessary to dispel confusion from the beginning student's mind.

In the case of Hittite, we have a duplex problem because it is written in two different scripts: cuneiform and pictograms. It was Bedřich Hrozný who established the Indo-European character of Hittite, thus setting Hittitology on its right course. The cuneiform script is Sumero-Akkadian and Hrozný did not have to figure out what the signs meant phonetically. The decipherment of Cuneiform Hittite resembles not the decipherment of Old Persian but rather that of Sumerian. The decipherment of pictographic Hittite (officially called Hieroglyphic Hittite) is, however, a true decipherment, for the phonetic values of the signs had to be worked out from scratch. There are such dialectal differences between Cuneiform and Hieroglyphic Hittite that our detailed knowledge of Cuneiform Hittite does not always clarify linguistic problems in the hieroglyphic variety.

To understand the fundamental difference between script and language, it may be of use to make a few observations on some modern forms of writing and speech. Finnish and Chinese are two languages equally unintelligible to the average English-speaking person. Finnish is written in familiar Latin characters, so that we have no problem knowing the sound conveyed by each letter. With Chinese, however, the pronunciation of the signs is as obscure as the meaning of the words and sentences, even if we could pronounce the text. Suppose we had to decipher both Finnish and Chinese. The magnitude of the two tasks would be different. With Chinese, script and language would have to be solved, with Finnish, only the language. Both tasks are of types that are generally called "decipherment," but they are, as we have seen, of different orders.

There is still another kind of decipherment: when the script is known but not the identity of the language, which, however, may turn out to be a known language once it is identified. For example, texts in Greek letters were found at El-Hofra in Algeria.[3] Since the language was not Greek and the town was Punic, it was immediately surmised that

---

3. For selected texts and bibliography, see C. H. Gordon, *Supplements to Vetus Testamentum* (Leiden: Brill, 1963), IX, pp. 22–23.

the texts were Punic. Their contents are so familiar from Punic inscriptions that no alternative view had to be considered. But it took three quarters of a century to identify the Semitic inscriptions in Greek letters from Crete. Shall we call such a feat a "decipherment" when in retrospect it seems so simple? To achieve it, in fact, it was necessary to decipher the parent language on Crete, which was Minoan. But is the identification and description of the Minoan language a decipherment? After all, the script is essentially the same as the Greek Linear B. But then again, should we even call the solution of Linear B a decipherment? For it turns out that the language and the system of writing are essentially the same as the Cypriot Greek texts written syllabically and deciphered by George Smith in 1872. By asking these questions we have answered them. The nuances and technical distinctions are endless, and we serve no useful purpose by hyperfinesse in our terminology. No two decipherments are exactly the same. We need only recognize that either scripts or languages or both can be known, partly known, or unknown. Moreover, even the identification of the language can be important because it can make the difference between intelligibility and mystery. When any person takes the first and critical steps to transform a category of mysterious inscriptions into intelligible documents by revealing their script or language, we shall call the achievement a decipherment.

Every problem in this book has been simplified. If we should follow step by step how each solution was achieved, it would be like recording every motion a baby made from birth until its first successful attempt at walking. We are concerned here primarily with success rather than with preparation or with failure.

It is exceedingly hard to establish priorities in every case. Usually somebody else anticipated someone in some way or other. Books are written about whether Columbus was really the discoverer of America. This book is not about whether Champollion really was the decipherer of Egyptian. We shall not wittingly cheat anyone of his due, but neither shall we be preoccupied with every "if" and "but" in our account. Decipherers, like all discoverers, want the credit for having got there first. Dated publications settle priority in one sense (and an important one at that), but what are we to think when A has published what he had already heard from B or found out concerning B's work? We shall touch on such problems for they are of historic interest, but we leave their detailed analysis to others.

SOLUTION OF CRYPTOGRAM ON PAGES 8 AND 10

The plain text is: "Ugarit was accidentally discovered by a peasant in nineteen hundred and twenty-eight. He plowed into a Mycenaean tomb and unwittingly opened up a new era of discovery."

Each letter was represented by the next one in the alphabet.

Cipher alphabet: A B C D E F G H I J K L M N O P Q R S
                   T U VW X Y Z
Plain alphabet: z a b c d e f g h i j k l m n o p q r
                   s t u v w x y

An experienced cryptanalyst, after determining the first few values, would detect the system (that is, each letter is substituted by the following letter in the alphabet). Determining the system usually precedes any successful decipherment.

2

THE DECIPHERMENT
OF EGYPTIAN

Some time around 3000 B.C.
writing was invented and developed in the Near East.
There is reason to believe that it first became established in
Mesopotamia, but the idea soon spread to Egypt.[1] The cuneiform of Mesopotamia has little obvious resemblance to
the hieroglyphs of Egypt, and yet their principles are so
similar that there must be a connection through stimulus
diffusion—the Egyptians did not copy the actual signs of
Mesopotamian writing but only applied the same basic

1. Henri Frankfort, *The Birth of Civilization in the Near East* (New York: Doubleday Anchor, 1956), pp. 121–37.

ideas. First, they established a large, but nonetheless limited, repertoire of pictographic signs. For example, they had not only a general sign for MAN but a number of other pictographs of men doing various things or in various states. Thus, there might be a man eating, but there would not be different signs for a man eating various kinds of food or different signs for a man engaged in various aspects of eating such as biting, chewing, or swallowing. If we draw each specific object or act, we are not writing but engaging in representational art. To be useful, any system of writing must limit its number of symbols.

The next principle (in both cuneiform and hieroglyphs) is that the pictograph can stand for the sound of what is drawn without reference to its meaning. To take some simulated English examples by way of illustration: the MAN pictograph could stand not only for "a man" but for the syllable *man*; even as the picture of a DATE could refer not only to "a date" but to the syllable *date*. Thus, the two pictographs MAN-DATE could be pronounced *man-date* and mean "a mandate." This is the most important and basic aspect of cuneiform and hieroglyphic writing; they are essentially phonetic systems even though as a rule the signs stood originally for words or ideas. As we follow the history of writing, we shall observe that the trend has been to abandon word-signs and concentrate on sound-signs.

The third principle common to Mesopotamia and Egypt is the use of determinatives, or signs that tell the category of the word. For example, there is no way of telling whether the isolated word spelled *sš* in Egyptian means "a scribe" or "a document." Accordingly, the Egyptians added the pictogram MAN when it means "scribe" but the pictogram SCROLL when it means "document." Thus,

ss, is "document," but ss, is "scribe."

Both cuneiform and hieroglyphs use phonetic complements to fix the sound of a sign. To take an Egyptian
example: a certain bird pictogram, usually identified as
GUINEA FOWL, has the reading nh. It can serve as the ideogram for the bird in question, but it can also be used as a
phonogram, in which case it may be both preceded and
followed by phonetic complements: ^{n}GUINEA FOWL^h,
which can be used to express words that have nothing
whatever to do with a bird and that we may represent
thus: $^nnh^h$. Now there is a verb $nh(i)$, "to pray," whose
meaning puts it in a category of words that the Egyptians
indicate by the determinative of a man pointing to his
mouth. The verb "to pray" can be written $^nnh^h$ followed
by that determinative:

. This kind of writing often makes Egyptian

easy to read and translate, for the word is written al-

phabetically (n-h) and syllabically (nh), and its

semantic category is indicated by the determinative .

It remains to add that numerals are often written ideographically down to our own times: I = "one"; II = "two";
and III = "three" are similar in appearance in cuneiform
(III), hieroglyphs (|), and Latin. All our numerical sym-
bols, indeed, are ideographic. Thus, 4 stands for the idea of
fourness; its pronunciation depends entirely on the language of the text in which it appears ("four" in English but
"quatre" in French).

From about 3000 B.C. until the end of the fourth century A.D., Egyptian was written in hieroglyphs in an unbroken tradition. The large number of signs and the numerous conventional spellings required long training for the chosen few who achieved literacy.[2] In the wake of Alexander's conquest, the Greek alphabet spread throughout the Near East including Egypt, where the Greek dynasty of the Ptolemies ruled and where there were many Greek settlers, especially in Alexandria.

In polyglot communities like Alexandria, where Greeks, Egyptians, and Jews lived side by side, it was common for the script of one linguistic group to be applied to the languages of the other groups. This is what happened in Egypt, where the Greek alphabet came to be used for writing Egyptian and, on a smaller scale, for Hebrew too.[3] The Greek letters did not have enough advantages over the Hebrew letters to threaten the latter with extinction. After all, the Hebrew script is alphabetic and with only twenty-two letters is a trifle easier to learn than the Greek alphabet of twenty-four letters. But Egyptian hieroglyphs were doomed to a slow death as soon as Egyptian began to be written in Greek letters. The old complex system could not compete with the new simple system.

With the rise of Christianity in Egypt, the process

---

2. The art of the scribe was the first stepping-stone on the way leading up to the highest positions in the pharaoh's government. In principle, it was open to any boy who demonstrated diligence and capacity in his studies. In this regard, Egypt was democratic.

3. Phoenician, Punic, and Eteocretan (which are related to Hebrew) are sometimes written in Greek letters. In the *Hexapla*, the Church Father Origen (c. A.D. 185–254) aligned two forms of the Hebrew Bible and four of its Greek translations. He provided the Hebrew both in Hebrew letters and in Greek letters. It is tacitly assumed that Origen invented the idea of writing Hebrew texts in Greek letters, but it is more likely that the Hellenized Jews sometimes wrote Hebrew in Greek characters much as the Phoenicians, Carthaginians, and Eteocretans expressed their kindred Semitic dialects in Greek characters.

whereby the Greek alphabet displaced the hieroglyphs for writing Egyptian was accelerated. Many of the early Christians were simple people without any education in classical Egyptian. The Egyptian Church adopted the popular device of writing Scripture and other necessary texts in Greek letters but in the Egyptian language.[4] Another factor played havoc with the very survival of hieroglyphic records: the latter were associated with paganism and frequently appeared in documents and on monuments depicting heathen gods. As a result, the early Church leaders in Egypt often stirred up their flocks against the ancient relics and incited them to acts of vandalism.

The Coptic Church still preserves the native Egyptian language written in Greek characters, so that we have an unbroken tradition of Egyptian texts spanning about five thousand years.

With the passing of hieroglyphic writing in Roman times, erroneous ideas concerning its nature gained currency. The pronouncements of an Egyptian named Horapollo, who in late antiquity wrote a treatise called *Hieroglyphica*, carried particular weight in Europe from the High Renaissance down to the early decades of the nineteenth century. Some of his meanings of hieroglyphic signs are correct, but his fanciful explanations obscured the true nature of the system. The fallacy that persisted from late Roman times to the nineteenth century was that each Egyptian hieroglyph conveyed some mystical or spiritual idea.

If any people in all of recorded history merits the de-

---

4. There are a few pre-Christian "Coptic" texts (that is, Egyptian texts in Greek letters) including incantations. Ignorant magicians often found it easier to inscribe spells alphabetically than in more complicated Egyptian Hieroglyphic, Hieratic, or Demotic scripts.

scription of "materialistic," it is the ancient Egyptians. They loved earthly life. Their cult of the dead is about as unspiritual as a religious concept can be. It aimed at achieving eternal life on a material plane. The body had to be preserved for a life full of the pleasures of this world with food, drink, servants, comforts, income, play, and games. No ancient Egyptian longed for a spiritual heaven with holy angels singing solemn hymns. Rather we know from tomb paintings that the Egyptians aspired to pleasures such as a family boat trip on the Nile to catch fish and birds among the bulrushes, or an entertainment of dancers and musicians. How such a fun-loving, materialistic people, whose character is revealed in their art as well as in the texts, came to be regarded as extraordinarily spiritual and mysterious illustrates how difficult it is for most people to take another culture on its own terms.

The mysterious Egyptians thus had a mysterious script full of mystical symbols ascribed to them. The decipherment of Hieroglyphic Egyptian required the replacement of the deep-seated notion of symbolism by the correct view that the main, though not the only, feature of the script is phonetic.

We may note at this juncture that while the decipherment of Egyptian has done away with the mysteries of the script, many still regard the ancient Egyptians as a philosophical, mysterious people whom we can never understand. Even the Pyramids are sometimes thought to embody profound secrets that we mere mortals can never fathom. Actually, no accomplishment of the human race is less mysterious or more successful. The Egyptians lived in houses of perishable materials because they viewed earthly life as perishable. They regarded the afterlife of men and the existence of the gods as enduring for ever. Therefore, they purposely selected stone as the building material of eternity for permanent structures associated with religion and the cult of the dead. From less spectacular beginnings, they developed the great Pyramids at Gizeh to endure for all time. No architects or builders have ever achieved their goals more efficiently and with such superb technique. Of all the Seven Wonders of antiquity, only the Pyramids are still standing—marvels to behold. How the technological fulfillment of so clear an aim came to be regarded as mysterious shows how inflexible the corporate human mind can be. A rational approach would have us view the Pyramid builders as great engineers rather than enigmatic mystery men of an inscrutable past.[5]

A Jesuit professor of philosophy, mathematics, and Oriental languages, Athanasius Kircher (1601–80), published in 1636 a study on Coptic in which he expressed his conviction that Coptic was a continuation of the ancient Egyptian language in alphabetic script. He was right, and the fact that he recognized was destined to provide the linguistic background for the decipherment of the hieroglyphs long afterwards when the time was ripe.[6]

A few scholars in the eighteenth century suspected the existence of phonetic hieroglyphs and made the correct suggestion that the cartouche (an oval enclosing groups of signs) was used to contain the names of kings and queens. One of the savants who made this important observation in 1797 was Johann Georg Zoëga. Then things began to move

5. See L. Sprague de Camp, *The Ancient Engineers* (Norwalk, Connecticut: Burndy Library, 1966), pp. 28–52.
6. For Kircher's own account of his pioneer work on Coptic grammar and vocabulary, see C. W. Ceram, *Hands on the Past* (New York: Alfred A. Knopf, 1966), pp. 154–58. Though Kircher was mistaken about the nature of hieroglyphic writing, he understood the significance of Coptic as the linguistic key to the language of the hieroglyphs.

faster. In 1798 Napoleon invaded Egypt, and in 1799 a contingent of his expeditionary force discovered the Rosetta stone, the key that started to unlock the secrets of the hieroglyphs.

The Rosetta stone is a black basalt slab that the French found in the course of rebuilding a fortification, in which it had already been re-used as building material.[7] The inscription that it bears in triplicate is a decree honoring the young Pharaoh Ptolemy V Epiphanes in 196 B.C. The text enumerates his good deeds and rules that his statues and copies of this decree shall be set up in all the temples throughout Egypt. The three versions are in two languages but in three scripts—Hieroglyphic Egyptian, Demotic Egyptian, and Greek. In remote antiquity, a cursive form of the hieroglyphs had developed into a script called Hieratic. In late Pharaonic times, Hieratic was further simplified and stylized into Demotic. Under the Ptolemies, Greek became an important language in Egypt. Accordingly, in the closing centuries of the pre-Christian era, bilingual texts in Greek and Egyptian were written and provided the Greek key for deciphering the forgotten scripts of ancient Egypt.

Anglo-French strife affected the fate of the Rosetta stone. A treaty forced its transfer to England, where it still is in the British Museum. A copy, made before the transfer, was delivered to the noted French Orientalist, A. I. Silvestre de Sacy (1758–1838). Though de Sacy did not make much headway with it, he showed it to the Swedish diplomat Johan David Åkerblad, who within two months made considerable progress with the Demotic version. Åkerblad's *Lettre à*

---

7. E. A. Wallis Budge, *The Rosetta Stone* (London: British Museum, 1913), reprinted 1922 and 1927.

M. de Sacy, published in 1802, identified all the names occurring in the Demotic by matching them with their counter-
parts in the Greek version and established the correct Demotic readings for "temples," "Greeks," and the suffix
meaning "he, him," or "his." Åkerblad rightly identified
this suffix and these two nouns with their Coptic forms.
(Though Demotic and Coptic are different in script, they
are quite close linguistically.) After this remarkable start,
Åkerblad was impeded from making further progress because of his erroneous idea that Demotic was exclusively
alphabetic. The readings he figured out were indeed alphabetic, but much of Demotic writing is not alphabetic.

The Rosetta stone is broken at the beginning (which
contains the Hieroglyphic version) and to a lesser extent at
the end (which contains the Greek translation). The Demotic, in the middle, while not intact, is the best preserved.
Therefore, the earliest efforts at decipherment were aimed
at the Demotic.

The next stride forward was made by an English physi-
cist Thomas Young, the author of the wave theory of light.
Exemplifying the best in the culture of his era, he was also
a doctor of medicine and wrote Latin with ease. Young was
versatile as well as learned and had the kind of mind that
is attracted to new and challenging problems. A copy of the
Rosetta stone fell into his hands in 1814. Young had be-
nefited from the results of Åkerblad's work but realized
that Demotic had so many signs that all of them could not
possibly be alphabetic. He also sensed the relationship between the Hieroglyphic and Demotic systems. The repetitions in the Greek version enabled Young to break each of
the three texts into their natural divisions and thereby to
isolate the individual words. Soon he compiled a vocabulary of eighty-six Demotic words or word groups matched

with their Greek translation. Most are correct. However, the phonetic values he ascribed to the Demotic signs are not as a rule felicitous, and accordingly his Coptic cognates are generally mistaken. In 1816 he announced further discoveries made from texts other than the Rosetta stone. He had matched long Hieroglyphic and Hieratic passages on papyri of the *Book of the Dead,* thus demonstrating the relationship between the pictorial and cursive forms of the writing. He proved (what others had previously suspected) that the cartouches enclosed royal names. In the papyri he noted variants in which certain signs could be replaced by other signs with the same phonetic values. Thus, Young established the principle of homophony. But Young's greatest contribution was his proof that the script was essentially phonetic and not philosophical, mystical, or symbolic.

Endowed with the spirit of a pioneer, Young was the first person to attempt the decipherment of the Hieroglyphic version of the Rosetta stone. Assuming that the hieroglyphs for writing names of Greek origin had to be phonetic, he matched the opening seven signs in the recurring cartouche with Ptolemaios (Ptolemy) in the Greek. The

Egyptian scribes group those signs thus:

However, we shall string them out in a straight line and assign numbers to them:

By matching these signs with Ptolemaios, Young proposed the following phonetic values: $1 = p$, $2 = t$, 3 (zero value),

4 = *ole*, 5 = *ma*, 6 = *i*, and 7 = *os*. We still render 1 and
2 the way Young did. He was wrong only about 3, which
has the value *o*. He was partly right regarding the rest: 4
has the value *l*; we now transliterate 5 as *m*, 6 as *y*, and 7
as *s*.

On another monument, Young correctly identified the

cartouche  as "Berenice." To simplify

the decipherment, we set the signs in a straight line and
number them:

Young's identifications were basically correct, but to facili-
tate matters, we shall assign the values we now know to be
right: 1 = *b*, 2 = *r*, 3 = *n*, 4 = *y*, 5 = *k*, 6 = ', 7 = *t*,[8]
8 = EGG (serving as determinative for feminine names).[9]

Young's demonstration that Egyptian writing is phonetic may be considered the rudimentary foundation of
scientific Egyptology. His correct conclusions were inevi-
tably mingled with errors, but this does not diminish his
achievement.

In 1815 at Philae J. W. Bankes excavated a granite obe-

---

8. In older stages of the Egyptian language, the ending of feminine substan-
tives was -*t*. In later times, due to a phonetic shift, the final -*t* was dropped in
the pronunciation, though it continued to be written as historic spelling (compare
the French *doigt* "finger" which is pronounced *dwa*, but the *g* and *t* are written
historically, recalling the Latin origin of the word, *digitus*). Accordingly, the final
-*t*, even though unpronounced, became a kind of graphic indicator of feminine
names (including foreign ones like Berenice and Cleopatra).

9. In effect we have two feminine determinatives (the -*t* and the EGG) without
any phonetic value here.

lisk inscribed with a Hieroglyphic inscription on all four surfaces. He also found nearby the base block on which it may possibly have been set. The block, which carries three different but related Greek inscriptions, names Ptolemy IX (Euergetes II) and his wife Cleopatra. None of the three Greek inscriptions corresponds to the Hieroglyphic inscription.[10] Nevertheless, the Hieroglyphic inscription includes a pair of cartouches, the first of which contains "Ptolemy" as inscribed on the Rosetta stone. In 1818 Bankes rightly took the other cartouche to contain the name of Cleopatra. The cartouche appears thus:

 We shall number the signs as

follows:

From the values established through the decipherment of the cartouches of Ptolemy and Berenice, we know that $2 = l$, $4 = o$, $5 = p$, and $8 = r$, while 10, which is the t sign, appears here only because the name is feminine and 11 is the determinative for feminine names. Accordingly, we have the following skeleton: $(1)L(3)OP(6)(7)R(9)$, and since the name is Kleopatra, $1 = k$, $3 = e$, and 6 and $9 = a$. There is an apparent problem concerning 7, which must equal t, even though a different letter for t occurs as the second sign in the name Ptolemy. Here we are confronted with the problem of homophony: different signs standing for the same sound.

10. E. A. Wallis Budge, *The Decrees of Memphis and Canopus*, 3 vols. (London: Kegan Paul, Trench, Trubner, 1904), 1: 135–59, for the Greek and hieroglyphic inscriptions on the Philae obelisk and base block.

In January 1822 the text with Bankes's identification was transmitted to Champollion, who soon afterwards made use of it in his decipherment of Egyptian. Unfortunately, the question of priority in such matters is a touchy subject, and we have anticipated the detailed decipherment of Cleopatra's name in order to stress Bankes's important identification made before the great breakthrough by Champollion, later in 1822.

The Frenchman destined to go far beyond Young's Egyptological discoveries was Jean François Champollion, born at Figeac in the Department du Lot, on 23 December 1790. He was a child prodigy who, at the age of eleven, decided that he would decipher the Hieroglyphic inscriptions. By his twelfth year he had begun the study of Hebrew and Arabic. As a teenager in Grenoble he studied ancient history, Coptic, and various scripts that might some day help him reveal the secrets of the Rosetta stone. He became professor of history at the Lyceum of Grenoble at the age of eighteen. For political reasons he lost a series of posts and in 1820 found refuge with his older brother, Jacques Joseph Champollion-Figeac, an archaeologist, who during his life ever encouraged Jean François and subsequently edited his posthumous publications.

So strong was Jean François's dedication to his Egyptological dream that he continued his Egyptian and Coptic studies unflaggingly during those stormy years. Equipped with a knowledge of Coptic and Egyptian history, he was ready to make his epochal contributions. Thanks to his study of the Rosetta stone and numerous other Egyptian inscriptions, he was able, in a brochure published in 1821, to transpose a Demotic or Hieratic or Hieroglyphic text into either of the other two. New texts were turning up, and there was enough source material to go ahead.

It is interesting to note that the outstanding Orientalist

of France, Silvestre de Sacy, tried to dissuade Champollion from attempting to decipher Hieroglyphic Egyptian and conceived a dislike for the student who was to eclipse him.[11] De Sacy, who was generous in such matters to Åkerblad and Young, lost no love on the most promising student he ever met. De Sacy was not only learned; he was also accomplished, but he lacked the qualities that a pioneer must have for scoring any primary breakthrough and was not big enough to encourage them in one of his own students.

Until nearly the end of 1821 Champollion did not extricate himself from the fallacy that the hieroglyphs were symbolic. So deeply ingrained was this error that he thought the lion, which merely stands for the letter *l*, in Ptolemy's cartouche symbolized war because *p(t)olemos* (the root of Ptolemy's name) is the Greek word for "war." At long last, on 21 December 1821, he abandoned the false notion of symbolism and concluded that the script must have phonetic signs. He realized this from a simple count, which showed that there are about three times as many hieroglyphs as words in the Greek, and therefore the hieroglyphs must include phonetic signs. He soon identified a number of Greek and Latin names and titles in their Hieroglyphic transcription, which enabled him to enlarge the list of phonetic values. Let us examine a few of them to see how the work was done:

The cartouche has these signs:

11. Budge, *Decrees*, p. 115 (for de Sacy's attempt to dissuade Champollion from attempting to decipher Egyptian) and pp. 68 and 70–71 (for de Sacy's denigration of Champollion's ability and intellectual honesty). On the surface, however, de Sacy and Champollion kept up appearances, so that in Champollion's hour of triumph, the younger man could pay open tribute to the older, who in turn could reciprocate with accolades in public.

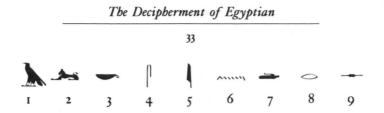

1   2   3   4   5   6   7   8   9

From the cartouches of Ptolemy, Berenice, and Cleopatra, we know that $1 = a$, $2 = l$, $4 = s$, $5 =$ a vowel like e, $6 = n$, $7 = t$, and $8 = r$. The skeleton of the name is Al-sentr-, which Champollion identified with "Alexander" in its Greek form "Aleksandros." Therefore, $3 = k$, $5 = a$ (even though it corresponds to e elsewhere), and $7 = d$ (though it corresponds to Greek t elsewhere), while 9 was another s (in accordance with the homophonous nature of the script).

The cartouche 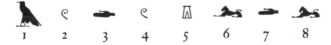 was now quite simple to identify.

1   2   3   4   5

$= kysrs =$ Kaisaros, the Greek form of "Caesar."

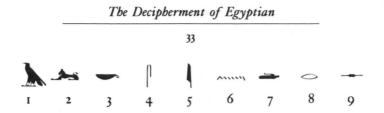

1   2   3   4   5   6   7   8

could now be read (a) (2) (t/d) (4) (k/g) (l/r) (t/d) (l/r). Since 2 and 4 are the same sign, Champollion correctly identified this group as *autokrator* (the Greek royal title) with 2 and 4 representing $w/u/o$.

Identifying 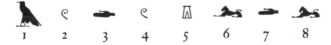 with Hadrian(os), we have

1   2   3   4   5   6
     t/d r n s

Champollion saw that 1 = *b* and 4 = some sound like *ia*.

In texts of the Ptolemaic and Roman periods, Champollion also identified the Hieroglyphic form of the royal Greek title Sebastos and of the names of Roman emperors such as Tiberius, Domitian, Trajan, and Antoninus as well as that of Germanicus. But all the decipherment was so far limited to the final stage of Hieroglyphic writing in Graeco-Roman times.

Until September 1822 Champollion still felt that perhaps only foreign names and titles were written phonetically. How were the native names of the old Pharaohs written? It was on 14 September 1822 that he succeeded in answering this question. Now that he could pronounce at least some of the signs, he turned to cartouches from the older periods, long before the Greeks and Romans. Thus, he noted

⦿ 𓏺 𓇳 𓏭𓏭 in a cartouche from a rock temple at Abu Simbel.

The last two signs he could read as -*ss* and the circle he identified as the "sun," which is pronounced *re* in Coptic. Could the series *Re-ss* stand for Ramses? All doubts were dispelled when he turned to another cartouche

(◯ 𓅠 𓏭𓏭) with the ibis of Thoth, so that this Pharaonic

name could only be Thothmes. Then in the Rosetta stone

Champollion noted that 𓏭𓏭 occurred in a group corre-

sponding to *genethlia* "birthday celebrations" in the Greek, tying in with Coptic *misi, mose* "to give birth." The battle was won. The phonetic system was clear, and the linguistic relationship of Hieroglyphic and Coptic Egyptian was established. From that day on, progress was assured, and the present stage of Egyptology—with all its great corpus of texts, dictionaries, grammars, histories, and innumerable special studies—was only a matter of time and labor.

On 27 September 1822 Champollion notified the Academy of Paris that in his famous *Lettre à M. Dacier relative à l'alphabet des hiéroglyphes phonétiques* he had succeeded in deciphering Egyptian. He read the letter before the Academy on 29 September but omitted many of his most important observations, including his identification of the names of Ramses and Thothmes. These and many other points were first published in his remarkable *Précis du système hiéroglyphique*, which appeared in 1824.

Much of the rest of his short life was spent gathering and studying material in Italy and Egypt. When he died on 4 March 1832 at the age of forty-one, he had established the character of Egyptian writing (differentiating ideograms, phonograms, and phonetic complements), the relationship between Pharaonic Egyptian and Coptic, and the foundations of Egyptian grammar and lexicography. Though he started with bilinguals, he eventually succeeded in translating unilinguals. His achievement is now self-evident, but for many years after his death his claims continued to be contested.

Champollion's brilliant discoveries met with great opposition, much of it acrimonious and personal, chiefly from scholars reared in the classical tradition, who resented the prominence given by these discoveries to an ancient "barbarian" nation.[12] Scholars belong to guilds held together by common opinions, attitudes, and methods. As a rule, innovation is welcome only when it is confined to surface details and does not modify the structure as a whole. For this

12. *Encyclopaedia Britannica*, 14th ed., s.v. "Champollion."

reason, new interpretations of a problematic word or verse may be applauded by the very academicians who will stop at nothing to discredit a breakthrough destined to touch off a major reappraisal of the entire field.

The opposition to Champollion's decipherment came to an end in 1866 when a bilingual stela, in Hieroglyphic and Demotic Egyptian and Greek, was discovered and published by a group of German scholars, including Richard Lepsius, who more than any other person marked the transition from the pioneering stage to the age of refinement in Egyptology. The text, known as the Decree of Canopus,[13] is the same kind of inscription as the Rosetta stone (the latter is sometimes called the Decree of Memphis). In 238 B.C. the priests, assembled at Canopus, promulgated the Decree, in which they enumerated the beneficent deeds of Ptolemy III and his wife Berenice and provided for honoring both of them and their ancestors. At the same time they established every fourth year as a leap year with an extra day. The style of the Decree of Canopus shed considerable light on the style of the Rosetta stone, which was written in the same tradition over forty years later. The long and almost perfectly preserved Decree of Canopus confirmed Champollion's decipherment and added further source-material to the rapidly growing field of Egyptology. Champollion's battle for acceptance was won, but not until the hero had been dead for thirty-four years.[14] His fame remains secure, while his detractors have gone to their well-earned oblivion.

The sequel is important but in the context of this book

13. Budge, *Decrees*, vol. 3, pp. 1–201.

14. We should not paint a completely gloomy picture of Champollion's struggle. He had friends as well as foes and lived to enjoy some recognition. He was made a Chevalier of the Legion of Honor and eventually, after considerable opposition, Professor of Egyptology at the Collège de France.

need not be dealt with at length. Adolph Erman guided Egyptology in the direction of its present status. He wrote a fine study of Late Egyptian (that is, the language after Ikhnaton in the fourteenth century B.C.), initiated the great Berlin dictionary of the Egyptian language, produced the standard work on life in ancient Egypt, and trained a generation of scholars who brought still greater finesse to Egyptology. The standard textbook is Alan Gardiner's *Egyptian Grammar*,[15] an amazing work in more ways than one. The author set out to compose a beginner's book with graduated exercises from Egyptian to English and from English to Egyptian. It is divided into lessons with grammatical topics illustrated profusely with selections from the whole range of the literature. The vocabularies are valuable, but the exhaustive and annotated sign-list is indispensable. What began as an elementary textbook ended up as the Bible of Egyptology. Studying Gardiner's *Grammar* is the foundation for a career in Egyptian; no scholar, no matter how advanced, ever outgrows his need of it.

Egyptian history is a vast subject in itself. Perhaps the best treatment is to be found in *L'Egypte* by E. Drioton and J. Vandier.[16] But an earlier treatment is in a way more important: Egypt is covered in E. Meyer's *Geschichte des Altertums*[17] (*History of Antiquity*), which also embraces Mesopotamia, Israel, Iran, Anatolia, and Greece. Meyer had a breadth of knowledge that is becoming more and more rare in an age of specialization. He knew not only the histories of the individual nations but perceived their rela-

15. Alan Gardiner, *Egyptian Grammar*, 3d ed. (New York: Oxford University Press, 1957).

16. E. Drioton and J. Vandier, *L'Egypte*, 4th ed. (Paris: Presses Universitaires de France, 1962).

17. Eduard Meyer, *Geschichte des Altertums*, 4 vols., 2d ed. (Stuttgart: J. G. Gotta'sche Buchhandlung, 1906–37), vols. 1–3.

tionships. Egypt is of great interest in its own right, but its importance lies in its impact on the origins and development of Western civilization. Moreover, the decipherment of Egyptian had an effect on the decipherment of the other scripts and languages that we are about to follow.

Before taking leave of Egyptian, it will be of interest to look at a Hieroglyphic text with its transliteration and translation. The selection is extracted from a stela of Sesostris III[18] and reflects the vigor that made Egypt great:

ir gr m-ḫt pḥ
He who desists after attack

sšm ib pw n ḫryw
is a strengthener of the enemy's heart.

qnt pw 'd
To be aggressive is brave

ḫst pw ḥm-ḫt
to retreat is cowardice.

ḥm pw m'c 'rw ḥr t'š.f
A real poltroon is he who is debarred from his own frontier

18. Gardiner, *Egyptian Grammar*, p. 361.

ḏr-ntt sḏm Nḥs r ḥr n ʿ
the Nubian hears so that he falls at a word

ʾin wšb.f dd ḥm.f
answering him causes him to retreat.

ʾd.t(w) r.f
If one is aggressive towards him

dd.f sʾ.f
he gives his back

ḥm-ḫt.(tw)
If one retreats

wʾ.f r ʾd
he falls into aggression.

n rmṯ(t) ʾis nt šft st
They are not people of worth

ḥwrw pw sḏw ʾibw
they are cowards broken of heart.[19]

19. For a knowledgeable and charming translation and interpretation of Egyptian literature, see Joseph Kaster, *Wings of the Falcon: Life and Thought of Ancient Egypt* (New York: Holt, Rinehart & Winston, 1968).

3

GROTEFEND'S
DECIPHERMENT
OF OLD PERSIAN

The same intellectual climate in Europe that led to the decipherment of Egyptian simultaneously produced the decipherment of cuneiform. In 1802, the very year that Åkerblad scored his success in reading parts of the Demotic version of the Rosetta stone, a young German high-school teacher cracked the system of Old Persian Cuneiform.

Cuneiform is not one script, but a variety of different

systems of writing with wedge-shaped signs (the Latin for "wedge, nail" is *cuneus*). Cuneiform was developed by writing on soft clay with a stylus that ended in a triangle, whence is the triangular nail head on all of the component parts of the signs. For certain kinds of texts, such as royal inscriptions on mountain walls, the scribes incised the signs with chisels. On neither soft nor hard materials did cuneiform lose its wedge-and-line character. To the end it shunned curves and never went through any stylistic transformation of the kind we see in the development of Hieroglyphic into Hieratic and finally into Demotic. During its three thousand years of history, the cuneiform signs became simplified and were formed with fewer wedges, but they never became cursive.

The earliest important language expressed in cuneiform was Sumerian, with both ideographic and phonetic signs, along with determinatives and phonetic complements much like Egyptian. The Semites of Mesopotamia, who are called the Akkadians, borrowed Sumerian writing to express their own Akkadian language. Later, other nations, such as Elamites, Hurrians, Hittites, and Urarteans, took over the same script from the Akkadians to write their own languages. But the Persians during the Achaemenian dynasty (the sixth to fourth centuries B.C.) devised a simplified system of writing using fewer than forty alphabetic and syllabic signs plus half a dozen ideograms.[1] This Old Persian resembles Sumero-Akkadian writing only insofar as both are cuneiform; no sign in the one can be pronounced or translated on the basis of any similar sign in the other.

At a number of Persian and Median sites, trilingual inscriptions on stone buildings and on mountain walls at-

1. For the historic background of ancient nations discussed in this book, see C. H. Gordon, *The Ancient Near East* (New York: Norton, 1965).

tracted the attention of European travelers. All three versions are in cuneiform, but unlike the trigraphic Rosetta stone, none of the three cuneiform scripts could be read. Accordingly, the decipherers of cuneiform had to undertake, so to speak, the solution of an equation with three unknowns and no knowns. It is therefore necessary for us to trace the rediscovery of the essential elements of information that led to the decipherment of Old Persian Cuneiform in 1802, which in turn made it possible to decipher Sumero-Akkadian Cuneiform and push back history in Western Asia by two millennia.

There are not as many references in ancient Greek literature to cuneiform as there are to Egyptian hieroglyphs. Herodotus, however, states that Darius set up two columns at the Bosphorus—one with Assyrian letters, one with Greek letters.[2] The *grammata assyria* ("Assyrian letters") of Herodotus can only mean cuneiform. But for all intents and purposes the very existence of cuneiform was forgotten in the mainstream of European culture.

In the Age of Discovery that followed the Renaissance, a succession of Europeans began to visit the Persian sites where the Achaemenian and later Persian rulers had left inscriptions and sculptures in the living rock. In 1472 Giosafat Barbaro was dispatched to Persia as the Venetian ambassador. He visited Persepolis (the capital built mainly by Darius and Xerxes),[3] the nearby site of Naqsh-e-Rustam (a veritable outdoor museum of Achaemenian and Middle Persian antiquities), and the earlier Achaemenian capital of Pasargade, where Cyrus the Great had ruled. It was not

---

2. A. D. Godley, ed. and trans., *Herodotus* (Cambridge, Mass.: Harvard University Press [The Loeb Classical Library], 1957), vol. 2 (4:87), p. 288.
3. In this book, "Darius" (521–485 B.C.) and "Xerxes" (485–465 B.C.) always refer to "the First" kings of those names.

until 1545, however, that Barbaro's *Viagi fatti da Vinetia alla Tana* was published.

The first European to write about the cuneiform inscriptions was Pietro della Valle, who discussed them in a letter sent from Shiraz in 1621 to a friend in Naples. The letter includes his copy of five Old Persian cuneiform signs.

Jean Chardin (1643–1713) visited Persepolis and other sites in 1666, 1667, and 1674, although his *Voyages* (published in Amsterdam) did not appear until 1711. He opposed the common view that cuneiform was not writing at all but simply decoration. Chardin was the first modern author to study the inscriptions carefully, to publish a complete text in all three versions (Old Persian, Elamite, and Babylonian), and to provide a good description of the Naqsh-e-Rustam texts. He decided, correctly, that cuneiform goes from left to right.

Engelbert Kämpfer (1651–1716), who visited Persepolis in 1686, described the signs as *cuneatae* "cuneiform," thus giving the script the name by which it is now known.

The man who made enough source material available for the decipherment of Old Persian was Carsten Niebuhr (1733–1815) from Danish Holstein. He was first drawn towards the study of mathematics, but he also devoted himself to Arabic. That language helped qualify him to join the expedition sent by Frederic V of Denmark in 1761 to explore Arabia. This assignment enabled him to travel in Egypt, Syria, Palestine, and Arabia as far south as Sanaa. In 1762 and 1763 several members of the expedition died. In 1764, Niebuhr and the expedition surgeon sailed for Bombay. During the voyage the surgeon died, leaving Niebuhr as the only survivor of the expedition. After spending fourteen months in Bombay, Niebuhr set out on a series of travels in Persia and Mesopotamia. Early in March 1765 he went to Persepolis, where he spent three weeks surveying the site, making ground plans of the buildings, and copying inscriptions. It was his clear copies that made the decipherment possible. In 1788 he published correct and complete copies of several important trilinguals of Darius and Xerxes, some long and some published for the first time. He recognized that three different systems of writing were involved.

In 1798, Olav Gerhard Tychsen (1734–1813), an Orientalist from Rostock, was the first to make use of Niebuhr's copies. He recognized that a divider separated words in the first system (which we now know to be the Old Persian) and correctly assumed that the systems of writing expressed three different languages.

In 1802 a Danish scholar, Friedrich Münter (1761–1830), correctly ascribed the trilinguals to the Achaemenian kings. He independently recognized the word divider in the first version and suggested it was alphabetic, while the second version was syllabic and the third ideographic. While not entirely correct, this observation was, on all three counts, a step in the right direction. Münter deduced from the parallel repetitions in the three versions that all three dealt with the same subject matter. He also spotted the signs designating "king" and "king of kings."

The successful and complete decipherment of Old Persian required the knowledge of some closely related language. We have seen how Coptic provided the linguistic data required for the recovery of the old Egyptian language. But the situation in Iran was not the same as in Egypt, where the native Coptic church still preserves the Egyptian language in Greek letters. When Alexander the Great destroyed the Achaemenian Empire (331–30 B.C.), Achaemenian civilization—script and all—was doomed.

Later, when the Parthians and Sasanians ruled Iran, they wrote the Persian language in letters derived from the Aramaic alphabet. It is true that the Zoroastrians of Iran preserved very ancient Persian writings, the Zend-Avesta, but with the Arab conquest, the Iranians were steadily converted to Islam, so that today there is only a tiny, but respected, Zoroastrian minority in Iran. The Zoroastrians who fled to India are now called the Parsees, a prosperous and educated minority that has retained its identity and perpetuated a knowledge of the ancient Zoroastrian scriptures in Persian. The situation required that European scholars master the Zend-Avesta from Parsee teachers in India and make that language available to the Orientalists who would some day elucidate the Old Persian cuneiform inscriptions.

Abraham Hyacinthe Anquetil-Duperron (1731–1801) went to India where he studied Persian under Parsee teachers and prepared a translation of the Zend-Avesta. On returning to France, he revised and published the translation in 1771, incidentally providing the linguistic basis for getting at the Old Persian cuneiform texts.

The towering figure in Oriental studies, however, was Silvestre de Sacy, who played a role, as we have seen, in the beginnings of Egyptology. In 1793 he published his *Mémoires sur diverses Antiquités de Perse*, in which he published some short Pehlevi (Middle Persian) inscriptions of the Sasanian kings at Naqsh-e-Rustam. By using the Greek version of bilinguals, he was able to decipher the Pehlevi original in which the king would call himself "A., the great king, the king of kings, the king of Iran and non-Iran, the son of B., the great king. . . ." We may now turn to the pioneer who used this and other collateral information to score the breakthrough.

The transliteration and translation of both texts will help the reader follow Grotefend's reasoning:

	TEXT 1	TEXT 2
1)	*da-a-ra-ya-va-u-sha* Darius	*kha-sha-ya-a-ra-sha-a* Xerxes
2)	*kha-sha-a-ya-tha-i-ya* king	*kha-sha-a-ya-tha-i-ya* king
3)	*va-za-ra-ka* great	*va-za-ra-ka* great
4)	*kha-sha-a-ya-tha-i-ya* king	*kha-sha-a-ya-tha-i-ya* king
5)	*kha-sha-a-ya-tha-i-ya-a-* *na-a-ma* of kings	*kha-sha-a-ya-tha-i-ya-a-* *na-a-ma* of kings
6)	*kha-sha-a-ya-tha-i-ya* king	
7)	*da-ha-ya-u-na-a-ma* of countries	

8) *vi-i-sha-ta-a-sa-pa-ha-ya-a*
of Hystaspes

9)

10) *pa-u-ca*
son

11) *ha-kha-a-ma-na-i-sha-*
i-ya
Achaemenian

12) *ha-ya*
who

13) *i-ma-na*
this

14) *ta-ca-ra-ma*
palace

15) *a-ku-u-na-u-sha*
built.

da-a-ra-ya-ca-ha-u-sha
of Darius

kha-sha-a-ya-tha-i-ya-ha-ya-a
of king

pa-u-ca
son

ha-kha-a-ma-na-i-sha-i-ya

Achaemenian.

Georg Friedrich Grotefend (1775–1853), a high-school teacher in Göttingen, loved to solve cryptograms. In 1802, when the challenge of deciphering ancient scripts was very much in the cultural atmosphere, Grotefend tried his hand at Old Persian. Although he was not an Orientalist, he had studied philology and had the knack of ferreting out the essential collateral information required for solving problems.

Inspired by de Sacy's translation of the royal Pehlevi formulas, Grotefend assumed that the latter followed an Old Persian tradition. He had correctly decided that the first version of the trilinguals should be in the native language of the Achaemenian kings. The Old Persian signary, which has fewer different signs than the other two, requires more signs to write the same text than the other two systems. In fact, there are sometimes as many as ten signs between word dividers in the Old Persian. All this led Grotefend to guess that the script was alphabetic (for it is more likely that words have ten alphabetic letters than ten syllables). Actually the Old Persian system is a compromise between an alphabet and a syllabary, but Grotefend was close enough to the truth to achieve a notable measure of success by comparing two different but typologically related inscriptions published by Niebuhr. The relation was clear to Grotefend from the recurrence of words and phrases in the same sequence. To bring this out, we shall align the two texts in parallel columns and indent the words that are identical in both texts. In normal English these texts are to be translated:

Darius, the great king, the king of kings, the king of countries, the son of Hystaspes, the Achaemenian, [is the one] who built this palace.	Xerxes, the great king, the king of kings, the son of King Darius, the Achaemenian.

Applying the Sasanian formula ("A., the great king, the king of kings, the king of Iran and non-Iran, the son of B., the great king . . . "), Grotefend saw in line 1 the name of the respective king and in lines 2–5 his title "great king, king of kings." Accordingly, in lines 2, 4, and 5 there is the word for "king"; the longer form in line 5 should contain the suffix of the genitive plural ("of kings"). The word in line 10 should mean "son," for the formula requires the king's paternity. Since in Text 2 the word for "king" occurs in line 9 (just before "son"), line 8 must contain the name of the king's father. In Text 2, the king's father is none other than the king (genitive) whose name appears as the king (nominative) in the first line of Text 1. But the name of the latter's father (Text 1, line 8) is not followed by the title "king." Therefore, Text 2 was written for the son of the king for whom Text 1 was written. But the king in Text 1 was not the son of a king. Who could the king in Text 2 be?

Grotefend decided on King Xerxes, son of King Darius, son of Hystaspes (for Hystaspes is never given the title of king by Herodotus). This conclusion is supported by the fact that "Darius" and "Xerxes" are of about the same length (six letters in Greek, seven in Old Persian), while "Hystaspes" is longer (nine in Greek, ten in the Old Persian genitive). Therefore, Text 1:1 contains the name "Darius" in the nominative and Text 2:8 contains the same name in the genitive, while Text 2:1 contains "Xerxes" in the nominative. Text 1:8 thus contains the genitive form of the name of Darius's father Hystaspes, who was not a king.

By operating with what he considered to be the Old Persian forms of Hystaspes, Darius, and Xerxes and by assuming that the script was an alphabet, Grotefend got the following phonetic values, which we shall compare with the transliteration currently used:

NAME	GROTEFEND'S TRANSLITERATION	CORRECT TRANSLITERATION
Hystaspes	*g o sh t a s p*	v^i *sh*^{a} *t*^{a} *a s*^{a}*p*^{a}
Darius	*d a r h e u sh*	*d*^{a} *a r*^{a} *y*^{a} *v*^{a}*u sh*^{a}
Xerxes	*kh sh h a r sh a*	*kh*^{a} *sh*^{a} *y*^{a} *a r*^{a} *sh*^{a} *a*

The correct (in the sense that it is now accepted) transliteration reckons with inherent vowels, which may or may not be disregarded in the pronunciation. When they are disregarded, the signs are used alphabetically as Grotefend assumed. Grotefend's absolutely alphabetic transliteration is no further from the correct one than our absolutely syllabic transliteration, and we should not consider it an error, especially as the work of the pioneer. Accordingly, from those three names alone he got the right phonetic values for *sh, t, a, s, p, d, r, u, kh*: nine signs, thus laying the foundation for reading the Old Persian inscriptions. He also identified the words for "king" and "great," and later, in 1815, he identified the name of "Cyrus" in an inscription from Murghab. This he was able to do after a British diplomat who knew Persia well, James Justinian Morier (1780–1849) identified the tomb at Murghab as Cyrus's. The native Persians had lost all memory of Cyrus who had made of them the world's greatest power, and they attributed his tomb to Madar-e-Suleiman (the mother of King Solomon).

Grotefend's task was more difficult than the decipherment of Egyptian, where an intelligible Greek translation provided the key. The decipherment of Old Persian was the work of a genius who sniffed out the few essential texts and facts to solve with directness and economy of material and time a problem that seemed incapable of a solution.

On 4 September 1802 Grotefend presented his paper with the solution to the Göttingen Academy. The Academy did not consider it worth publishing and printed only a short notice about it. Silvestre de Sacy displayed more intelligence by writing up in 1803 a full account of Grotefend's decipherment, including both of the Old Persian texts complete with transliteration and translation, for Millin's *Magasin Encyclopédique*. Another detailed report was published in Arnold Heeren's rather broad study, *Ideen über die Politik, den Verkehr und den Handel der vornehmsten Völker der alten Welt (Ideas on the Politics, Relations and Trade of the Leading Peoples of Antiquity)*. But in general Grotefend's decipherment was disregarded by the Orientalists, who should have recognized its importance and built upon it.

Bilingual confirmation of Grotefend's decipherment was pointed out in 1823 by J. A. Saint Martin (1791–1832) on a vase that had been published in 1762 by Count Caylus. The vase bears a quadrilingual inscription in Old Persian, Elamite, Babylonian, and Hieroglyphic Egyptian. Champollion had read the Egyptian. The text says "Xerxes, the Great King," every word of which had been read by Grotefend on the Persepolis inscriptions in 1802. But this bilingual confirmation of the decipherments of Old Persian and Egyptian did not dispel the misgivings or indifference of the run-of-the-mill specialists who so often on such occasions are too obtuse to know that something highly significant has happened in their own field.

Forty years after Grotefend's death, the world of learning made amends to the pioneer. In 1893 his manuscript was recovered and published in full, a landmark in the history of cuneiform studies. The refusal of the Göttingen Academy to publish it nine decades earlier is unfortunately not a unique act of stupidity. Academies, committees, editorial boards, and the like are sometimes composed of men who are too "down to earth." To them the work of genius may be indistinguishable from folly.

In identifying the sounds of twelve Old Persian signs

(one third of the phonetic symbols), Grotefend had laid the foundation of the decipherment. The reason he could not make more headway was twofold. First, he had no access to the great trilingual of Darius at Behistun. Secondly, he was not enough of an Orientalist to master the growing field of ancient Persian studies. The completion of the task of deciphering Old Persian required a knowledge of the Zend-Avesta and the related Sanskrit language. The nascent discipline of Indo-Iranian linguistics had an important contribution to make.

Rasmus Christian Rask (1787–1832), a Danish authority on Zend and Pehlevi, studied Grotefend's decipherment and concluded that the language of the Achaemenian inscriptions was closely related to Zend Persian with both coming from approximately the same age. In 1826 Rask read correctly the genitive plural suffix -ānām occurring in the phrase "king of kings" and thereby established the right values for the *na* and *-ma* signs.

In 1836 the Zend scholar Eugène Burnouf (1801–52) published his *Mémoire sur deux inscriptions cunéiformes*, in which he succeeded in identifying two more signs correctly. His knowledge of Zend and Sanskrit enabled him to translate several Old Persian words, of which the most important and useful was *a-da-ma* (adam) "I (am)." Burnouf realized the importance of the Zend-Avesta for Old Persian studies, and when his commentary on the Yaçna (a liturgical work that forms the third part of the Avesta) appeared in 1834, its value was recognized by the scholars in Europe engaged in the decipherment of the Old Persian inscriptions.

In the same year (1836) that Burnouf's *Mémoire* was published, Christian Lassen (1800–76) published *Die altpersischen Keilinschriften*, which covered much of the same ground as Burnouf. Both scholars happened to be friends and were in touch with each other. But Lassen had a good idea which produced outstanding results. Remembering that Herodotus tells us that Darius inscribed the names of the nations that made up his armed forces upon the pillars he set up by the Bosphorus,[4] Lassen thought such a list ought to appear among the Persepolis texts. He found one that mentioned twenty-four proper names, of which he identified nineteen. This enabled him to increase the number of signs with known phonetic values to twenty-three. Knowing the Avestan forms of the names was of prime value to Lassen. From his command of Sanskrit, he recognized that in Old Persian (as in Sanskrit writing), short *a* was not written after the normal series of consonants. That is, what Grotefend read as *t, d, r, kh, sh, s,* and so forth, may also stand for *ta, da, ra, kha, sha, sa,* and so forth. The *a* sign follows only to indicate long *ā*; that is, *da-a* stands for *dā*.

In 1837 E. E. F. Beer (1805–41) identified two more signs, while Eugène Vincent Stanislas Jacquet (1811–38) identified six (including the two independently found by Beer). Although these two men were not able to improve on the translations of Burnouf and Lassen, the new values they found helped Iranologists add to the vocabulary of Old Persian.[5]

The importance of the decipherment of Old Persian goes far beyond the limited corpus of the Achaemenian inscriptions in the Persian language. Through the phonetic evidence of the proper names, the Elamite and Akkadian versions were deciphered in the trilinguals. Once Akkadian was deciphered, it opened up the vast literatures in Ak-

---

4. Godley, *Herodotus*, p. 288.
5. Many of the details concerning the decipherment of cuneiform are covered by E. A. Wallis Budge, *The Rise and Progress of Assyriology* (London: Martin Hopkinson & Co., 1925). A brief account is given by David Kahn, *The Codebreakers* (New York: Macmillan, 1967), pp. 912–14.

kadian and Sumerian from Babylonia, Assyria, and the
entire Near East. And it was only a matter of time for the
unlocking of Hittite and other literatures written in the
Akkadian system of cuneiform. As a result, our historical
and philological knowledge has been widened enormously.

Grotefend's decipherment was destined to be eclipsed by
the work of a different kind of pioneer, Rawlinson, about
whom we shall read in the next chapter. But Grotefend's
achievement stands out as a gem of brilliant simplicity.
Great thinking is often direct and naïve. Such was Grotefend's decipherment in 1802.

4

RECLAIMING THE SUMERO-AKKADIAN LEGACY

The towering giant among the pioneers in cuneiform studies is the Englishman Henry Creswicke Rawlinson (1810–95). During his school days at Ealing, he was especially interested in the Greek and Latin historians. At the same time, he was good in athletics. His intellectual and physical abilities combined to equip him for the great task that lay ahead. In 1827 he was sent by the East India Company to India, where he studied Persian,

Arabic, and Hindustani and gained enough proficiency to become the interpreter as well as paymaster of the First Bombay Grenadiers in 1828. In 1835 he was selected for service in Iran as military adviser to the shah's brother, who was governor of the province that included Kirmanshah (in Iranian Kurdistan).

Though Rawlinson may have heard about what Grotefend and other scholars had achieved in Europe, there is no reason to suspect that he had any specific information about the readings of any signs in any of the Old Persian inscriptions until the close of 1836. His indebtedness to his predecessors is in the nature of "stimulus diffusion" rather than of outright borrowing.

On his way to Kirmanshah he heard about two cuneiform inscriptions on Mount Elvend, near Hamadan. The natives still call the texts "Ganj Nameh" ("Treasure Story") because of the tradition that they tell where treasure is hidden. From these two inscriptions, which he copied in 1835 and checked in 1836, he concluded that one had been written for Darius, son of Hystaspes, and the other for Xerxes, son of Darius, and he arrived at much the same results that Grotefend had long before, by treating similar material along similar lines.

After arriving in Kirmanshah, Rawlinson heard about the huge inscription with reliefs on the mountain wall at Behistun, about twenty-two miles east of the city. He visited the site often in 1835 and began to copy the text. Towards the close of 1836, he learned from Colonel Taylor, the British Resident in Baghdad, of Grotefend's accomplishment in deciphering Old Persian. But Rawlinson stated that Grotefend's values were of no use to him, because he himself had already identified more signs than had Grotefend. In any case, Rawlinson's claim to fame is not for making the first decisive steps in the decipherment, for Grotefend anticipated him by a third of a century. Rawlinson's great achievement hinges on his rediscovering, copying, and deciphering the Behistun inscription, which is longer and more important than all the other Achaemenian trilinguals combined. At the risk of life and limb, Rawlinson spent years in copying the text and then used it not only for the Old Persian but also for deciphering the most important of the versions, the Babylonian. Moreover, he did not keep all the material for himself but let others share in the decipherment. The text tells how Darius quelled rebellions at home and abroad and proclaims the might and extent of the Empire. It is full of personal and geographical names that provided Rawlinson with the phonetic values of the signs. It also contains plenty of narrative that revealed the grammar and basic vocabulary of Old persian.

In 1836 and 1837 Rawlinson succeeded in translating the first two columns of the Old Persian section of the Behistun inscription, totalling nearly 200 lines. He wrote up his account of the text with transliteration, translation, and notes for the Royal Asiatic Society in 1837. It reached London early in 1838. Edwin Norris (1795–1872) sent a copy of it to the Société Asiatique in Paris so that Burnouf and other French scholars might read it. They were so impressed that they elected Rawlinson an honorary member of the Société and sent him Burnouf's *Mémoire* of 1836 and the book on the Yaçna of 1833. It was on his paper of 1837, together with a supplement written in 1839, that Rawlinson based his claim of virtually completing the decipherment of the Old Persian script and not, as is sometimes stated, on his fuller "Memoir" of 1846.[1]

---

1. E. A. Wallis Budge, *Rise and Progress of Assyriology* (London: Martin Hopkinson & Co., 1925), p. 51.

By identifying the names of Hystaspes, Darius, and Xerxes in the Ganj Nameh texts, Rawlinson obtained the phonetic values of thirteen signs, which we now transliterate (with the inherent vowels represented by raised letters) $d^a, a, r^a, y^a, v^a, u, sh^a, kh^a, v^i, i, t^a, s^a$, and p^a. But Rawlinson remembered that, according to Herodotus, Xerxes stated he was the son of Darius, the son of Hystaspes, the son of Arsames, the son of Ariaramnes, the son of Teispes, the son of Cyrus, the son of Cambyses, the son of Teispes, the son of Achaemenes.[2] While there were only three royal names in the Ganj Nameh inscriptions, Rawlinson suspected that in the Behistun inscription there might be more. He was right, for the Old Persian version starts thus: "I am Darius the Great King, King of Kings, . . . King of Countries, son of Hystaspes, grandson of Arsames, and Achaemenian." Darius the King says, "My father was Hystaspes, Hystaspes' father was Arsames, Arsames' father was Ariaramnes, Ariaramnes' father was Teispes, Teispes' father was Achaemenes." Accordingly, when Rawlinson found a-r^a -sh^a-a-X where "Arsames" was expected, he knew that $X =$ m (now transliterated m^a). Since a-r^a-i-y^a-a-r^a-m^a-Y corresponded in the genealogy to "Ariaramnes," the final sign was n (now n^a). In Z-kh^a-a-m^a-n^a-i-sh^a-i-y^a, "Achaemenes," the first sign, could not represent a (for another sign was already identified as a), so Rawlinson correctly took it to stand for ha. The length and character of the Behistun inscription enabled Rawlinson to go further than others could with the decipherment of Old Persian. Copying the text required athletic prowess and considerable daring; deciphering it required knowledge, intelligence, and perseverance.

---

2. A. D. Godley, ed. and trans., *Herodotus* (Cambridge, Mass.: Harvard University Press [The Loeb Classical Library], 1957), vol. 3 (7:11), p. 332.

In 1839 the Afghan War broke out, and in 1840 Rawlinson was appointed Political Agent in Kandahar. He organized, trained, and led a unit of Persian calvary, with which he scored a victory in the battle outside Kandahar on 29 May 1842. His military career ended by the close of that year, and he turned down other opportunities so that he could return to Baghdad, where he would not be too far from Behistun and other sources of cuneiform texts. Colonel Taylor retired from his post as Political Agent in Turkish Arabia, and Rawlinson succeeded him in 1843 with headquarters in Baghdad. With two companions he returned to Behistun early in the summer of 1844 and completed copying the Persian and Elamite versions. The tale of how the job was executed with ropes and ladders, by gaining access to the narrow ledges made by the ancient scribes and sculptors, by shifting positions adroitly to evade death—is a hair-raising tale that Rawlinson himself has described.[3]

In 1847 Rawlinson returned to Behistun to copy the Babylonian version, which is even harder to reach. It can be copied from below with the aid of a telescope, but Rawlinson wanted to make a paper squeeze of the text—which was particularly important because that surface was being worn away by erosion from the trickling of rain water. This task was too arduous even for Rawlinson, but he found a "wild Kurdish boy" who by climbing like a human fly, fastening pegs in rocky clefts, attaching ropes from which he swung from position to position, "by hanging on with his toes and fingers to the slight inequalities on the bare surface of the precipice," and other feats of daring and skill, set up a sort of painter's ladder and, under Rawlinson's direction, made the squeeze of the Babylonian version

---

3. His account is republished by Leo Deuel, *The Treasures of Time* (Cleveland: World Publishing Co., 1961), pp. 125–31.

that was destined to open up the whole field of Assyriology.

The Old Persian inscriptions are of historical and linguistic interest in their own right, but their great importance lies in the fact that their translation was the key to the Babylonian version of the trilinguals that clarified the vast epigraphical treasures of Babylonia and Assyria. Although the proper names provided the pronunciation of the signs, it was the knowledge of Avestan Persian and Sanskrit that enabled Rawlinson and other European scholars to work out the vocabulary and grammar in detail and to translate the texts correctly. So close is Old Persian to the language of the Avesta that the etymological method was used with considerable success. Words with exactly the same sound and meaning occur often enough in these two closely related forms of ancient Persian. Later in the nineteenth century, fragments of the Aramaic translation of Darius's Behistun text were discovered at Elephantine, in Upper Egypt.[4] Aramaic is a well-known Semitic language, but those fragments merely confirmed what the decipherers had achieved without benefit of bilingual aids: Old Persian had been completely solved the hard way.

As a sample of Old Persian we may note this prayer in cuneiform, excerpted from an inscription of Darius at Persepolis, with its transliteration, normalization, and translation:[5]

𒊹	𒈠	𒀀	𒈠	/	𒊹	𒁕	𒄩	𒅀	𒀀	𒌋	𒈠	/
i	ma	a	ma	/	da	ba	ya	a	u	ma	/
imām					dahyāum							
this					land							

---

4. Included in Arthur E. Cowley, *Aramaic Papyri of the Fifth Century B.C.* (London: Oxford University Press, 1923).

5. For the Old Persian inscriptions, see R. G. Kent, *Old Persian: Grammar, Texts, Lexicon,* 2d ed. (New Haven: American Oriental Society, 1953).

a u ra ma za da a / pa a tu u
Auramazdā pātuv
may Ahuramazda protect

va / ha ca a / ha i na a ya a
hacā haināyā
from (hostile) army

/ ha ca a / du u sha i ya a
hacā dushiyārā
from famine

ra a / ha ca a / da ra u ga a
hacā draugā
from the lie

"May God protect this country from foe, famine and falsehood."

The second language of the Achaemenian trilinguals is Elamite. Unfortunately, Elamite is not related to any well known language, and so etymology is of little help. Yet we know the meaning of the Elamite version because it is a translation of the Old Persian in the trilinguals, and one could not ask for a better bilingual key.

Since the Elamite version uses III signs, the script was recognized as a syllabary. The absence of word dividers made the analysis more difficult, but, as Grotefend noted in 1837, male personal names are preceded by a vertical wedge, following the Sumero-Akkadian tradition.

Niels Ludwig Westergaard (1815–78), who copied texts at Persepolis and Naqsh-e-Rustam in 1843, had the distinction of being the first copyist at those sites who understood what he was copying. He not only worked on proper names in the Elamite version but was also the first to transliterate an Elamite passage. Further progress had to await the publication of the Elamite version of the Behistun text by Edwin Norris of London in 1853, which increased the number of names read from forty to ninety. Thereby most of the phonetic values for the Elamite syllabic signs were established. Since the meaning of the text was supplied by the Old Persian text, a grammar and lexicon could be worked out. However, our linguistic comprehension of Elamite is still lagging behind our highly refined knowledge of Old Persian and Babylonian, because Elamite is virtually isolated linguistically. Moreover, Elamite never became important outside of western Iran.

A lot of hard and honest work has gone into Elamite, but its decipherment followed from the real pioneer work on the Old Persian, while the great importance of the trilinguals emanated from the decipherment of the Babylonian version. Realizing this, Rawlinson gave up his work on the Elamite and concentrated on the Babylonian version. The same may be said of the two other outstanding pioneers in Assyriology, the Irishman Edward Hincks (1792–1866) and the Frenchman Jules Oppert (1825–1905). These gifted scholars had already made contributions to the progress of deciphering Old Persian. Hincks, who happened to be an Anglican clergyman, also played a role in the decipherment of Egyptian, in which he recognized the function of determinatives.

Before the decipherment of Babylonian, it was known that the Babylonian version of the Achaemenian trilinguals was related to texts of Mesopotamia, examples of which had become known in Europe during the eighteenth century. Thousands of cuneiform inscriptions, on clay and on stone, were now to be unearthed by a succession of pioneer archaeologists. The head of the French vice-consulate at Mosul, Paul-Emile Botta, in 1843 began to excavate at Khorsabad, an Assyrian capital of Sargon of Assyria, who vanquished the northern kingdom of Israel in 722 B.C. Then in 1845 the Englishman Henry Austen Layard began to excavate at the still more important Assyrian capital of Nineveh.[6] These and other excavators filled the museums of Europe, such as the Louvre and the British Museum, with the inscriptions and art of Mesopotamia. Accordingly, it was evident that the third (Babylonian) section of the Achaemenian inscriptions was by all odds the most significant one, as Rawlinson and others recognized.

Matching the proper names in the Persian and Babylonian versions made it possible to work out the phonetic values of the Babylonian signs, but the process was long and arduous because of the complexities of the Babylonian system of writing. First of all, Babylonian has over 300 signs. The determinatives and ideograms, which are perfectly clear and helpful today, posed innumerable problems for the pioneers who were trying to make sense of them.

Moreover, Babylonian writing is characterized by both polyphony and homophony. A polyphonous sign has more than one phonetic value; thus, the TAR sign can be read (depending on the context) *tar, kud, ḫas, sil,* and *gùg.* Just as context tells us to pronounce *s* as the *sh* in "sugar" or in "sure" (and if we pronounce it *s* in this word, we would be saying "sewer," which has a very different meaning), the ancient scribes (like the modern Assyriologists) knew what

6. For a recent account, see Deuel, *Treasures,* pp. 99–124. Layard's own account, *Nineveh and its Remains,* 2 vols. (New York: George Putnam, 1849), is not only important but has a charm that no discriminating reader will want to miss.

value to ascribe to polyphonous signs, depending on the context. The script is also characterized by homophony; different signs with the same pronunciation. Thus, there are no fewer than nine entirely different signs with the value of *a*. (Compare *g, j, s*, and *z* with the sound of *zh* in "rouge," "Jacques," "pleasure," and "azure.")

There are still other peculiarities in Akkadian writing. In addition to signs to be read as *ba, bi, bu, ka, ki, ku*, and so forth, following the consonant-vowel pattern, and as *ab, ib, ub, ak, ik, uk*, and so forth, following the vowel-consonant pattern, there are others like *bab, ban, buk, kap, kan, kub*, and so forth, following the consonant-vowel-consonant pattern. Therefore, a word like *na-ar-ka-ab-tu*, (chariot), can also be spelled *nar-ka-ab-tu, na-ar-kab-tu*, or *nar-kab-tu*. Moreover, the scribes often enjoyed showing off their educations by writing the same word in different ways in the same inscription.

In 1850 Rawlinson, after successfully translating a fairly long historic text in Akkadian, admitted that after he had mastered every Babylonian sign and word that could be ascertained on the trilinguals, he was more than once on the verge of abandoning his work when he tried to apply his knowledge to the Assyrian inscriptions. It takes an Assyriologist who knows the material to sympathize with and understand the magnitude of Rawlinson's frustrations, which repeatedly brought him to the verge of despair.

In the 1840s Grotefend identified the names of Darius, Xerxes, Cyrus, and Hystaspes in the Babylonian texts. He also recognized a group of signs on bricks from Babylonia as the name of Nebuchadnezzar, although he could not read the individual signs that comprised it.

In Sweden, Isidor Löwenstern correctly advocated the Semitic character of Akkadian in 1845. The close relationship of Akkadian to well-known languages such as Hebrew and Arabic made it possible to use the etymological method successfully, provided that it is controlled by the simultaneous use of the contextual method. It was therefore only a matter of time until Akkadian lexicography and grammar were worked out with the high degree of refinement that typifies them today.

Hincks grasped the nature of Babylonian writing when, in 1850, he stated that no sign ever stood for a consonant alone but only for a whole syllable. It was he who recognized that the syllables were of three types (*ba, ab, and bab*). Hincks also realized that a sign could be polyphonous, and, for that matter, the same sign could serve as an ideogram, a syllable, or a determinative. He moreover identified a number of determinatives including those that indicate gods, countries, and cities.

The excavator Botta discovered that the same word might be written ideographically or syllabically. He noted that in the inscriptions from Sargon's palace, variants of the same text confronted him with the same word or name written briefly via an ideogram and spelled out at greater length syllabically. To take a simple example: the Akkadian word for "king" is *sharru*, which is usually written with the single KING ideogram, but it could be spelled out *sha-ar-ru* with three signs. Important contributions can be made by amateurs (and Botta was not a professional orientalist or philologian) at an early stage of a subject when everything is yet to be done, and the pioneering spirit can by itself produce useful results. Today Assyriology is so highly developed that a newcomer, no matter how brilliant, cannot hope to add anything valuable to Assyriology before learning the subject at the modern level. A tyro can hardly identify a new sign, a new word, or a new grammatical form that is not in the published sign-lists, dictionaries, or grammars. Real pioneering is not at home in highly developed disciplines.

By the middle of the nineteenth century, pioneers like Rawlinson and Hincks were able to read and translate Akkadian texts. During the three thousand years of cuneiform writing, the script had changed considerably. Moreover, in one and the same period different styles of script were used for different purposes. For instance, the Code of Hammurapi is written in archaic characters on a stone stela, whereas a much simpler form of the signs appears on the clay tablets from Hammurapi's reign. There are also geographical and chronological differences in Sumero-Babylonian writing. A scholar might be perfectly at home in the Akkadian cuneiform of the Achaemenian period yet unable to recognize the same signs in their earlier and more complicated forms two millennia earlier. Hincks clarified the matter when he identified as duplicates two inscriptions, one in Old Babylonian and the other in Neo-Babylonian characters.

The achievement of the pioneers was far from generally recognized. Scholars accustomed to texts in well-known languages and in familiar alphabets, like Latin and Greek, could not always take in their strides the complexities of Akkadian cuneiform with its ideograms, polyphony, and homophony. To settle the matter, the Royal Asiatic Society of London took a dramatic step suggested by William Henry Fox Talbot, a mathematician and the inventor of talbotype photography, who had become deeply immersed in Assyriology. It happened that in 1857 Talbot, Rawlinson, Hincks, and Oppert were all in London. Each was given a copy of a cylinder of Tiglathpileser I that had just been discovered, with instructions to work on it independently and submit their solutions sealed. When their communications were unsealed and opened, it was found that their interpretations were in essential agreement, with the result that the decipherment of Akkadian was not only in fact accomplished but also generally recognized. Even so, not all the denigration and sniping were over. In 1876, A. von Gutschmid attacked the decipherment so virulently that a productive Assyriologist, E. Schrader, felt obliged in 1878 to defend the subject against the attack. What E. Meyer says of Von Gutschmid can be applied to most of the destructive critics who have opposed any of the sound decipherments: "Such distrust concerning the reliability of the foundations of the decipherment would have vanished immediately, if critics like V. Gutschmid had taken the trouble to learn the first elements of the script."[7]

To convey a more concrete notion of how Babylonian was deciphered, we shall examine a few assorted texts to illustrate various aspects of the evidence.

The names and the meaning of the following Babylonian text of Xerxes were supplied by the decipherment of the Old Persian section (cited as Text 2 on page 46) of the same trilingual (with the phonetic symbols now used by Assyriologists, such as *š* for "*sh*" and *ḫ* for "*kh*"):

| *m* ḫi | – *ši* – | ꜣ | – | *ar* | – | *ši* | KING (= *šarru*) |
| Xerxes, | | | | | | | king |

| GREAT*ú* (= *rabû*) | KING (= *šar*) | KING*pl* (= *šarrâni*) | SON (= *mâr*) |
| great, | king | of kings, | son |

7. Eduard Meyer, *Geschichte des Alterums*, 2d ed., 4 vols. (Stuttgart: J. G. Gotta'sche Buchhandlung, 1909), vol. 1, 2, pp. 308–09.

^m *da* – *a* – *ri* – *ia* – *a* – *mus̆* KING (= *s̆arri*)
of Darius,   king

^m *a* – *ḫa* – *ma* – *an* – *nis̆* – *s̆i* – ’
Achaemenian

"Xerxes, the great king, the king of kings, son of King Darius, the Achaemenian."

In the transliteration, determinatives and phonetic complements are raised. Thus, ^m precedes male names; ^{pl} indicates plurality; ^ú means that the word it follows ends in -*u*. The ideograms are in capital letters. It is interesting to note that this text gives almost no evidence for the Akkadian language, for apart from the names, the words are written ideographically.

The complexities of the script were felt by the ancient scribes themselves. The scholars of Assyria and Babylonia compiled sign-lists, grammatical tables, and other school texts that have been instrumental in reconstructing the ins-and-outs of the subject.

Because so many tablets were found in the nineteenth century in the Assyrian capitals, particularly at Nineveh, dating to the eighth and seventh centuries B.C., the Assyrian script of that period was adopted as the standard in Assyriological publications. The important library of Assurbanipal (669–29? B.C.) at Nineveh contained such a wealth of texts that the choice of the script of the Sargonid kings of Assyria to serve as the norm was logical. However, about two thousand years of Sumero-Akkadian literature preceded the Sargonids of Assyria. To illustrate the kind of change that took place in a millennium, we shall compare a law of Hammurapi (No. 102 in his Code) as written about

1700 B.C. (on the left) with its transcription in the Assyrian signs of about 700 B.C.:

šum-ma DAM-GÀR (= *tamkārum*)
If a merchant

a-na ŠAMÁN-LAL (= *šamallim*)
to a tradesman

KUBABBAR (= *kaspam*) *a-na ta-ad-mi-iq-tim*
silver as a favor

it-ta-di-in-ma
has given,

a-šar   il-   li-   ku
where he went

bi- ti- iq-tam
loss

i-   ta-   mar
he has seen,

qá- qá- ad KUBABBAR (= kaspim)
the principal of the silver

a-na DAM-GÀR (= tamkārim) ú-ta-ar
to the merchant he shall return.

Paraphrasing this law for the sake of clarity, we are to understand, "If a moneylender lends money[8] to a trader without interest, and the trader's enterprise runs into a loss, the trader need only return the principal because there are no profits to share."

The interesting thing about this law is the term qaqqad-, which means "principal, capital" invested for profit, dividends, or a stipulated rate of interest. Literally, qaqqad- means "head"; the spread of the institution of investing capital for dividends or interest from Mesopotamia, via the merchants of Babylonia and Assyria abroad, has left its mark on the capitalist terminology of the West. In West Semitic, Demotic, and Greek, the word for "capital" is derived from a word meaning "head." Latin too reflects the same terminology, for caput means not only "head" but also "principal, capital." Indeed, our words for "capital" and "capitalism" are derived from caput. The simplest and most basic definition of capitalism is "an economic system which encourages the investment of capital for dividends or interest." The seeds of this system were planted and spread by

8. It is legitimate to use the word "money" in order to convey the sense of the passage. Coinage, however, was not invented until the seventh century B.C. in Lydia. Hammurapi (c. 1700 B.C.) speaks of "silver" with a value determined by the weight and quality of the metal.

Sumero-Akkadian businessmen. This is instructive because it illustrates that our culture as a whole reflects its Near East origins; our indebtedness is not limited to a few specialized areas such as religion, the alphabet, and literature. The foundations of our pure sciences and of our economic system are no less rooted in Mesopotamia and the other lands whose antiquities are being opened up by the decipherments.

The reader may have asked himself why the Babylonian scribe who wrote Hammurapi's Code wrote the ideogram KUBABBAR, "silver," when he wanted it to be pronounced *kaspum* "silver," in the excerpt above. It happens that KUBABBAR is the Sumerian word for "silver," and at every turn we see the great impact of Sumerian culture on the Akkadians—in religion, art, and writing—in short, in virtually everything.

In 1850 Hincks discovered that the Babylonian script had been devised for another language, and Oppert gave that language the name we use to designate it: Sumerian. The Akkadians regarded it as their classical language and therefore taught it in their scribal schools. To do this, they compiled bilingual vocabularies, bilingual grammatical exercises, interlinear translations, and so forth. For example, there are syllabaries in three columns. The center column lists signs with their Sumerian values on the left and their Akkadian values on the right. One such syllabary includes a section with the numerical ideograms for 10, 20, 30, 40, 50 as follows:[9]

9. From a syllabary in Friedrich Delitzsch, *Assyrische Lesestücke* 5th ed. (Leipzig: Hinrichs, 1912), p. 109.

SUMERIAN	SIGN	AKKADIAN
𒌋 *ú*, "ten"	◁ X	𒌋 "ten" *e-še-ru*, "ten"
ni-iš, "twenty"	◁◁ XX	*eš-ra-a*, "twenty"
e-eš, "thirty"	◁◁◁ XXX	*še-la-šá-a*, "thirty"
ni-in, "forty"	◁◁◁ (over) ◁ XL	*ir-ba-a*, "forty"
ni-in-nu-u, "fifty"	◁◁◁ (over) ◁◁ L	*ḫa-áš-šá-a*, "fifty"

The following selection from a comparative Sumero-Akkadian grammatical text illustrates the kind of material that the ancients themselves have left us for reconstructing the inflections of the Sumerian language:[10]

SUMERIAN	AKKADIAN	ENGLISH TRANSLATION
in-lá	*iš-qú-ul*	"he weighed"
in-lá-eš	*iš-qú-lu*	"they weighed"

10. Ibid., p. 112.

SUMERIAN		AKKADIAN	ENGLISH TRANSLATION
in-lá-e		i-ša-qal	"he will weigh"
in-lá-e-ne		i-ša-qa-lu	"they will weigh"
in-na-an-lá		iš-qú-ul-šu	"he weighed it"
in-na-an-lá-eš		iš-qú-lu-šu	"they weighed it"
in-na-an-lá-e		i-ša-qal-šu	"he will weigh it"
in-na-an-lá-e-ne		i-ša-qá-lu-šu	"they will weigh it"

In spite of the clear evidence for the Sumerian language,
its very existence was denied by many scholars. The Assyrians and Babylonians were at least known from the
Bible and the classics. But it was too much for some to
believe that Assyro-Babylonian civilization was
thoroughly indebted to a still older culture whose very
name had not survived in any Hebrew,[11] Greek, or Latin
document. But how could anyone deny the straightfor-
ward evidence? The negators can always find a way. Their
leader was Joseph Halévy, who maintained that Sumerian
had never existed as a real language but was a kind of

11. It is possible, but not certain, that Hebrew šinᶜār (Genesis 10:10, and so forth)
"Babylonia" is the Hebrew phonetic approximation of "Sumer."

ancient cryptographic system invented by the priests and scribes for keeping secrets within their own circle.

Assyriology made a profound impression on Western intellectual life because of its direct bearing on Old Testament history. The invasions of Assyrian and Babylonian kings are recorded in the Bible. Disbelief in the traditional literatures had grown to such proportions that many educated men decided that Old Testament history had been largely invented by Hebrew authors to hoodwink a gullible world. But then came the cuneiform historical documents with the official Mesopotamian version of the very same campaigns described in the Bible. It soon became clear that biblical history is indeed history. Today our ancient-history books draw on the evidence of newly deciphered texts, as well as on Hebrew and classical sources. We no longer depend on the Bible alone for biblical history concerning Mesopotamian kings named in the Bible, such as Tiglath-pileser, Sargon, Sennacherib, Esarhaddon, and Nebuchadnezzar. We possess their own cuneiform annals to confirm, modify, and above all, to supplement the Hebrew accounts.

This kind of text gave comfort to the conservative members of various religious bodies, but there was another kind of text that was disturbing to them. Scripture, especially in the early chapters of Genesis, contains myths and legends that unsophisticated believers mistook for history. The legend of Noah is a profound document that inculcates the basic attitude necessary for a united mankind. It teaches us that all men, regardless of nation, race, or language, are brothers, descended from one man (Noah) and his wife. It leads up to the remarkable tenth chapter of Genesis, which views the entire known world as a single community of related nations. These are big ideas that mankind must absorb (as attitudes, not as historical or anthropological facts) and apply if our planet is to be worth living in. But believers who naïvely regarded the Deluge as an historical event were shaken upon learning that the same story (albeit devoid of the aspect we have just noted in the Genesis version) circulated among the ancient Mesopotamians long before Genesis was written.

The British excavations at Nineveh unearthed the great library of Assurbanipal (669–29? B.C.), including fragments of the Gilgamesh Epic, a twelve-tablet masterpiece unmatched in epic literature until the Homeric epics in Greek. At the British Museum, a self-educated young man named George Smith (1840–76) took a special interest in the Gilgamesh tablets. He was familiar with the Bible and had a predilection for the early books of the Old Testament. His knack for piecing together broken tablets enabled him to make many valuable joins that helped reconstruct the texts. Smith picked up all he could from his more formally educated associates at the Museum and absorbed what could be learned from books and articles. As a result he developed into a first class Assyriologist and, because of his special interest in the Gilgamesh tablets, became the outstanding authority on Babylonian myths and legends.

In 1872 Smith observed that the eleventh Gilgamesh tablet narrated a flood story unmistakably connected with the tale of the Deluge in Genesis. Floods are well-nigh universal in legend and myth; but the Genesis and Gilgamesh floods are related, and there is no doubt that the Hebrew depends on the Babylonian rather than vice versa. In both accounts, the flood hero builds the ark and waterproofs it with pitch in accordance with divinely given instructions. Representatives of human, animal, and bird life are taken aboard to perpetuate the various species. The hero determines the availability of dry land after the flood by sending out a series of birds until one does not return, thereby indicating the recession of the waters. The ark lands on a mountain, where the hero gratifies the god(s) with sacrifices. The god(s), smelling the sweet savor, promise(s) never to afflict man with another flood.

Smith's discovery was announced and immediately captured the imagination of secular and religious intellectuals in Europe and America. This was roughly the age of Darwinism, and the Western world was divided between rationalists eager to tear down Scripture and fundamentalists who wanted to confirm Scripture and repudiate science. Then, as now, there were also the enlightened few who cherished tradition and simultaneously wanted to learn from science and discovery whatever they could to enhance their understanding.

A fragment of the eleventh tablet was missing. Smith estimated its length to be fifteen lines. He wanted to go to Nineveh and dig it up. The *Daily Telegraph* subsidized his expedition in exchange for the publication rights. Smith went to Nineveh and in a matter of days found the very fragment (it was seventeen lines long) he had come for. Never has an archaeologist dug for something so specific or found it so quickly.[12]

George Smith's discovery of the Babylonian parallel to Noah opened up a whole era of uncovering Mesopotamian parallels to the Old Testament: an era which is far from over. The religious background of Western Europe and America was such that chairs in Assyriology were founded on both sides of the Atlantic. Germany took the lead in refining Assyriology and in training native and foreign

12. See Deuel, *Treasures*, pp. 132–43.

students. For a time, American Assyriologists went to Germany for their doctorates, starting with the pioneer American Assyriologist, David Gordon Lyon of Harvard University.[13]

Assyriology flourishes more than Egyptology, in the United States and elsewhere, largely because the importance of Assyriology for biblical studies was stressed and the subject was thereby made relevant for Western culture at a level understood in America and Europe. Egyptology is just as important as Assyriology for biblical studies, but Egyptologists have tended to specialize more narrowly on their own subject, which has therefore remained in relative isolation. In the 1920s, an Egyptian book of wisdom attributed to a sage called Amenemope was discovered and published. Its closeness to a section of the biblical Book of Proverbs is so obvious and detailed that it started a movement that almost brought the Old Testament and Egyptology together. Unfortunately, the chief exponent that emerged, the late A. S. Yahuda, was not the man who could crystallize the union of the two fields. He wrote lucidly and well, knew the Hebrew Bible intimately, and had studied Semitics and Egyptology under the best authorities in Germany, but he was not a critical philologian and his work became discredited—and still remains so—because academicians so often fail to separate the wheat from the chaff.

In important matters, Yahuda was often way ahead of his detractors. He recognized that the correct background for any given part of the Bible must come from the land where that episode is set. The parts dealing with Joseph and Moses are to be understood against Egyptian background, the Book of Esther against Persian background, and so

13. One of the present writer's Assyrian teachers at the University of Pennsylvania was George A. Barton, who had been trained by Lyon at Harvard.

forth. He rightly understood that the Genesis tales with Mesopotamian background were not (as most scholars then believed) late borrowings from the Exilic period (after 586 B.C.) but from a very early time generally called the Patriarchal Age. What neither he nor his critics realized was that the earliest Hebrews did not have to be in Mesopotamia to absorb their Akkadian background; the latter had permeated the entire Levant, including Palestine, before the Hebrews had conquered the land. Yahuda got no recognition for his labors and insights; instead he reaped a harvest of abuse and ostracism.

While Egyptology tended to remain self-contained, the revelations of Assyriology led to a powerful "Pan-Babylonian" movement throughout the West, especially in Germany. It was sometimes called "Babel and Bible," implying that virtually everything in the Old Testament stemmed from Mesopotamia. Around the turn of the century, even the ordinary man in the street in Germany was concerned with *Babel und Bibel.* [14] It ran its course and eventually became discredited because of its one-sidedness, but actually not even its greatest advocates fully appreciated the magnitude of Mesopotamian influence on the Hebrews as well as on the entire East Mediterranean. It turns out that Babylonian was the international language used throughout the East Mediterranean—in Egypt, Palestine, Lebanon, Syria, Anatolia, and Cyprus. Babylonian inscriptions of the second millennium B.C. have even been found in Greece at Thebes and on Cythera.

The upshot of the matter is that the faith of our fathers

14. The controversy it provided is reflected in Friedrich Delitzsch, *Babel and Bible: Two Lectures on the Significance of Assyriological Research for Religion* (Chicago: Open Court Publishing Co., 1903). Delitzsch had to defend himself against invective and vilification that he abhorred "with profound disgust" and described as "mental and moral depravity" (p. 167).

and grandfathers was shaken simultaneously by the discoveries of science and archaeology. Darwin and his peers came up with evidence that was seen as challenging the accuracy of the Creation in Genesis. George Smith and a whole generation of Assyriologists produced translations of tablets that were regarded as undermining the uniqueness of the Hebrew Deluge and the other early biblical narratives. We and our children still suffer from the insecurity and confusion that resulted from the twofold assault on tradition.

The simple truth is that Genesis cannot be used as a textbook on geology, any more than *The Origin of Species* can take the place of the Ten Commandments or the Sermon on the Mount. Any enlightened person needs science and tradition, each in its own place and taken on its own terms. There is no more contradiction in this than in the statement that to live we need air as well as food.

The enlightened man must know about the decipherments and the literatures that they have unlocked. Otherwise, one can succumb to various fundamentalisms, such as the view that Homeric epic was an Olympian miracle revealed to a hitherto benighted mankind or that a revelation on Sinai gave the first ray of light to a world engulfed in barbarism. To the contrary, we know that the Bible and Homer are both culminations of highly developed and literate ancient civilizations. We can understand the Bible and the classics only against the background of their foundations as recorded in the cuneiform and Egyptian texts and in the monuments associated with those texts. The value of the decipherments lies not so much in the solving of riddles but in the contents and nature of the texts that they have opened. As a result of archaeological discovery and the decipherments, we not only perceive the prehistory of the Bible and the classics, but we also see how they towered above their predecessors and contemporaries.

In Germany, Friedrich Delitzsch (1850–1923) did much to raise the level of Assyriology to new heights and trained a host of disciples. His Assyrian dictionary remained the best until the great *Chicago Assyrian Dictionary*, which is being published in fascicles. His *Assyrische Lesestücke* was the best reading-book for half a century and is still useful. Arthur Ungnad, who composed the most lucid Akkadian grammar, was another outstanding Assyriologist; in its revised edition this concise book still provides an excellent means of learning the structure of the language.[15]

Bruno Meissner published a two-volume work called *Babylonien und Assyrien*,[16] covering the whole range of ancient Mesopotamian civilization. Newer books have appeared that should be used for bringing the subject up to date,[17] but they have not replaced *Babylonien und Assyrien* as the authoritative work. Meissner also prepared on cards the materials for an Akkadian lexicon (under the title *Akkadisches Handwörterbuch*), which one of the ablest living Assyriologists, Wolfram von Soden, has processed for publication; it, too, appeared in fascicles. Less exhaustive than the huge *Chicago Assyrian Dictionary*, which is the product of complex teamwork, the Meissner-Soden lexicon is of more manageable proportions and has inner consistency because it was compiled by a single authority and carefully revised by another, neither of whom was subject to outside pressures for alterations or compromise. The final fascicle was issued in 1981. Von Soden is

---

15. Arthur Ungnad's Akkadian grammar was revised by Lubor Matouš and published under the title of *Grammatik des Akkadischen*, (Munich: Beck, 1964).

16. B. Meissner, *Babylonien und Assyrien*, 2 vols. (Heidelberg: C. Winter, 1920–25).

17. For example, H. W. F. Saggs, *The Greatness That Was Babylon* (New York: Hawthorn Books, 1962), and A. Leo Oppenheim, *Ancient Mesopotamia: Portrait of a Dead Civilization* (Chicago: University of Chicago Press, 1964).

also the author of the detailed grammar of the Akkadian dialects, which is indispensable for the advanced student.[18]

In spite of the abundant Sumerian materials—including bilinguals and school texts—Sumerian linguistics lags behind Akkadian because Akkadian is Semitic, whereas Sumerian has no close relationship to any other known language. A Frenchman, François Thureau-Dangin, rendered an outstanding service in translating royal Sumerian unilinguals in 1907 so accurately that he provided a basis for all future work.[19] His German counterpart, Arno Poebel, was often in polemic conflict with him on details. Poebel's Sumerian grammar, published in 1923,[20] was a great step forward in systematizing the rules of the Sumerian language. On the other hand, the transliteration he employs is often incomprehensible to the present generation of cuneiformists. Thureau-Dangin's system of transliterating Sumero-Akkadian has prevailed. Poebel migrated to America and ended his career at the Oriental Institute of the University of Chicago. It was there that he trained two of the foremost living Sumerologists, Samuel Noah Kramer and Thorkild Jakobsen.

The best available grammar of Sumerian is limited to the texts of one ruler, Gudea of the city-state of Lagash, c. 2000 B.C., whose inscriptions constitute the most classical expression of Sumerian. Adam Falkenstein (1906–66) of Germany produced a comprehensive study of Gudea's texts with a detailed grammar of them, covering the phonology,

18. W. von Soden, *Grundriss der akkadischen Grammatik* (Rome: Pontifical Biblical Institute, 1952); reissued as a 2d ed. with a supplement (an "Ergänzungsheft") in 1969.

19. F. Thureau-Dangin, *Die sumerischen und akkadischen Königsinschriften* (Leipzig: Hinrichs, 1907).

20. A. Poebel, *Grundzüge der sumerischen Grammatik* (Rostock: privately printed by the author, 1923).

morphology, and syntax.[21] While the general meaning of the texts is clear, numerous passages are still interpreted differently by the top Sumerologists, nor is there always unanimity on grammatical analysis. Sumerian is the world's first great classical language; its impact through Akkadian has been enormous and still reverberates in our culture.

The Akkadian scribes, trained as they were in bilingualism from the very start because of their Sumerian heritage, were (unlike the Egyptians) generally ready to use their script for other languages and to compile bilingual, trilingual, and even quadrilingual texts for didactic purposes. An important people in the Akkadian sphere during the entire second millennium were the Hurrians. For a while there was a Hurrian kingdom called Mitanni in Northwest Mesopotamia. During the early part of the Amarna Age (the late fifteenth and early fourteenth centuries B.C.), when the Pharaohs in Babylonian corresponded with other rulers all over the civilized world, the Mitannian king Tushratta wrote a very long letter in Hurrian, as well as other letters in Babylonian, to Amenophis III. Tushratta was a quite repetitious correspondent, so that even though his Hurrian letter is not a bilingual, we know from his Akkadian letters the things he had on his mind. Besides, the script of the Hurrian letter is identical with the script of the Akkadian correspondence and is therefore pronounceable. The ideograms and determinatives provide welcome clues as to the meaning of many words.

The slow and imperfect decipherment of Hurrian is due to the exotic affinities of the language, which is unrelated

---

21. A. Falkenstein, *Grammatik der Sprache Gudeas von Lagaš*, 2 vols. (Rome: Pontifical Biblical Institute, 1949–50). Volume 1 covers the script and morphology; volume 2, the syntax.

to Semitic, Indo-European, Sumerian, and almost everything else. Meanwhile, bilingual inscriptions in Akkadian and Hurrian have turned up and also school texts that list Hurrian words parallel to their equivalents in Sumerian, Akkadian, or Ugaritic (two tablets listing words in all four languages in parallel columns have been found at Ugarit). Hurrian texts written in the Ugaritic alphabet have also been found. And yet the Hurrian letter of Tushratta remains the chief source of our knowledge of the language. By working with phrases containing known personal names and by matching up Hurrian and Akkadian phrases in the Amarna Letters, Hurrian vocabulary, grammar, and syntax have made some definitive progress. For instance, *ᵐni-im-mu-u-ri-a-aš* LAND *mis-sí-ir-ri-e-we-ni-eš iw-ri-iš* means "Nimmuria [one of the known names of Amenophis III], King [*iwriš*] of Egypt" and *ᵐar-ta-ta-a-maš am-ma-ti-iw-wu-uš* means "Artatama, my grandfather" (known as such from Tushratta's Akkadian letters). The following are among the expressions in Akkadian and Hurrian that can also be paired: Akkadian GOD*ᵖˡ li-me-eš-še-ru-uš,* "may the gods allow it" = Hurrian GOD*ᵖˡ e-e-en-na-šu-uš na-ak-ki-te-en;* and Akkadian *ki-i-me-e a-mi-lu-ú-tum* GOD *Šamaš i-ra-'-am-šu,* "as mankind loves the Sun" = Hurrian *i-nu-ú-me-e-ni-i-in* GOD *Ši-mi-gi tar-šu-an-niš . . . ta-a-ti-a.* In the latter pair, Hurrian *inu* = Akkadian *kīmē,* "as"; Hurrian *Shimigi* = Akkadian *Shamash,* "Sun (god)"; Hurrian *taršu-anni* = Akkadian *amēlūtum,* "mankind"; Hurrian *tat-* = Akkadian *ra'āmu,* "to love."[22]

---

22. See Johannes Friedrich, *Extinct Languages* (New York: Philosophical Library, 1957), pp. 79–81. The second edition of the original German book *Entzifferung verschollener Schriften und Sprachen* (Heidelberg: Springer-Verlag), appeared in 1966. A later comprehensive treatment of the language is Frederick William Bush, *A Grammar of the Hurrian Language* (Ann Arbor, Michigan: University Microfilms, 1965).

Towards the end of the nineteenth century, scholars such as Peter Jensen and Daniel G. L. Messerschmidt laid the foundations for interpreting Hurrian texts by matching such Akkadian and Hurrian equivalent phrases and then proceeding from the known Akkadian to the unknown Hurrian. Bit by bit many lexical and grammatical details have been squeezed out of numerous texts, but the specialized nature of the latter and the lack of relationship with a well-known linguistic family leave us with an inadequate knowledge of the language. We have, for example, grammars of Hurrian that give learned discussions of grammatical features, but when a new Hurrian text is found, it is only with the greatest difficulty that the best-qualified scholars can eke out the meaning of even a fraction thereof.

Armenia nurtured an ancient civilization. Its iron and copper mines were important in a world that needed metals for its technology and daily life. The biblical flood story has Noah's Ark landing on the Mountains of Ararat[23] (Urartu, as Armenia is called in the cuneiform records). This can mean only that Armenia was considered an important center when the Genesis Deluge account was formulated. Located in the mountains where Turkey, the Soviet Union, Iran, and Iraq now meet or come near one another, Armenia was in a position to resist the onslaught of the Assyrian armies more successfully than many of the other targets of Assyrian imperialism. Indeed, from the ninth through the seventh century, B.C., Urartu was the most effective rival of Assyria, and until 714 B.C., when Sargon of Assyria invaded and weakened Urartu, the Urarteans were the rivals of the Assyrians in claiming to be the world's leading power.

23. Genesis 8:4.

Around 1000 B.C. the Hurrians disappeared from the scene at large except in Urartu, where they held on down to the general upheaval associated with the Scythian invasion around 600 B.C. Urartean is fairly closely related to Hurrian. There are about 200 Urartean inscriptions from Turkey, Iran, and the Soviet Union, including two Akkadian-Urartean bilingual stelas. Additional clues to the meaning come from the ideograms and determinatives that are found in the Sumero-Akkadian system used for writing Urartean. The limited scope and character of the texts, combined with the fact that the language is related only to the imperfectly known Hurrian, leave us with an all-too-sketchy lexical and grammatical picture of Urartean.[24] Work on the subject is fully justified, no matter how lean the pickings may be. Urartu, after all, was one of the two leading nations in the Near East for over a century. Too little is known about it. Whatever we can learn about the Urarteans and their language is likely to be more important than the casual observer might expect.

Apart from Sumerian and Akkadian themselves, the most important language written in their script is Hittite, which is discussed in the next chapter.

---

24. Friedrich, who has done detailed work on Urartean, gives a succinct account of its partial decipherment in *Extinct Languages*, pp. 81–82.

5

CUNEIFORM AND
HIEROGLYPHIC HITTITE

The history, language, and literature of the Hittites are of exceptional interest. Hittite is the oldest recorded Indo-European language; it is related to Sanskrit, Greek, Latin, English, and most of the other well known languages of Europe. In the second millennium B.C., the Hittites were a major force on the international scene and in the fourteenth and thirteenth centuries rivaled, and sometimes eclipsed, Egypt and the Mesopotamian powers as the world's leading nation. Early in the twelfth century, when the whole East Mediterranean was in a state of turmoil, the Hittite capital of Hattusas (now near Boğazköy in central Turkey) was destroyed by invaders and never rebuilt.

In retrospect, it is surprising that this great empire, which was very much in the mainstream of world history, had been for all intents and purposes lost to human memory. There are references to the Hittites in Scripture,[1] but it was the decipherment of Egyptian and cuneiform that provided so much information on the Hittites that orientalists realized how important the Hittites were. In a temple at Karnak there is inscribed a text dealing with the treaty (c. 1280 B.C.) between Ramses II and the Hittite king Hattusilis III. Many Assyrian texts refer to Hattu ("Hittite land"), as the West is sometimes called, including Syria and Palestine. The tablets found in Egypt at Tell el-Amarna since 1887 include letters exchanged between the Egyptian and Hittite kings. Gradually it was realized that the Hittites had not only been a major Near Eastern power but had also dominated the land bridge joining the cuneiform and Semitic spheres to the Greeks in Ionia.

The rediscovery of the Hittites was based on scattered bits of curious evidence that did not fit into the conventional scheme of things.[2] By 1870 Egyptian hieroglyphs and Mesopotamian cuneiform had left the impression that, before Hebrew and Greek history, the Near East had only two main elements: Egyptian and Assyro-Babylonian. But very modest indications of a third culture had come to

1. Genesis 10:15; 23:3, 5, 7, 10; Exodus 3:8, 17; Deuteronomy 7:1; 20:17; Joshua 3:10; Judges 3:5; Ezekiel 16:3, 4, 5; and so forth.
2. The routine scholar tends to be concerned with "normal" phenomena in keeping with accepted opinion. The pioneer is attracted to atypical data whose investigation may lead to new horizons.

light. In 1812 the Anglo-Swiss explorer Johann Ludwig Burckhardt (1784–1817) noticed a stone in Hamath, North Syria, bearing pictographs quite unlike Egyptian hieroglyphs. No one paid much attention to this until two American diplomats found it and four similarly inscribed stones in Hamath in 1870 and published their findings in 1872.[3]

The man who first associated the Hamath hieroglyphs with the Hittites was the Reverend Archibald Henry Sayce (1846–1933), Professor of Comparative Philology and Assyriology at Oxford University. Exemplifying nineteenth-century scholarship, he was grounded in classics and Hebrew. The spirit of intellectual adventure had led him to the expanding frontiers of history and to the languages and literatures that were emerging during the century of the great decipherments.

In due time, texts with the same hieroglyphs as those found at Hamath turned up elsewhere. With the exception of lead scrolls inscribed in a cursive form of the same script, found at Assur, the evidence is limited to seals and to stone inscriptions from Anatolia, North Syria (and now also Thebes in Greece). Sayce reasoned that those two contiguous areas (Anatolia and North Syria) had once been ruled by the Hittite kings. Specifically, the hieroglyphs inscribed on stone were found at Yazilikaya (near Boğazköy); at the pass of Karabel (near Smyrna); at Ivriz (in the Taurus Mountains); and at the North Syrian sites of Hamath, Aleppo, and Carchemish. The most impressive are in the outdoor mountain shrine of Yazilikaya, which seemed to be

---

3. See the accounts by Ernst Doblhofer, *Voices in Stone* (New York: Viking Press, 1961), pp. 150–53; P.E. Cleator, *Lost Languages* (New York: John Day, 1959), pp. 115–16; and especially William Wright (1837–99), in C. W. Ceram, *Hands on the Past* (New York: Alfred A. Knopf), 1966, pp. 270–76.

the national shrine, near what accordingly appeared to be the national capital buried under a great mound not far from the village of Boğazköy. Thus, in a few vestiges of the undeciphered Hittite monuments, Sayce perceived the presence and extent of the Hittite Empire. His views were, of course, hotly contested. Most scholars like to have a great preponderance of evidence, and even then there are many who will not face the facts. Outstanding innovators like Sayce work differently; they sense the significance of odd bits of material and then generalize from them. If the theory is correct—and the reconstruction is as important as they claim—further evidence will be found. Sayce had the satisfaction of discovering the Hittite Empire and of having his pioneering views corroborated, beyond his hopes and dreams, in his lifetime.

The Amarna tablets, found in 1887 and thereafter, began to fill the gaps in our knowledge, for they include references to the Hittites and a letter written by the great Hittite King Shuppiluliuma to the Pharaoh. But the Amarna tablets also include two letters in Hittite from Arzawa in Asia Minor.[4] The script is the Akkadian of the Amarna Age and can be pronounced. The ideograms and names are clues to the meaning. The Norwegian Assyriologist J. A. Knudtzon came out in 1902 with a publication on the Arzawa letters in which he correctly concluded that the language was Indo-European. He noted, for example, that *e-es-tu*, which from context has to mean "may it be," is the Indo-European *esto* "may it be." This important discovery was right, and if Knudtzon had had the courage of his

---

4. The best edition is still J. A. Knudtzon, *Die El-Amarna Tafeln* (Leipzig: Vorderasiatische Bibliothek, 1907–15). A later edition is S. A. B. Mercer, *The Tell el-Amarna Tablets*, 2 vols. (Toronto: Macmillan, 1939). In both editions the Arzawa letters are texts #31 and #32.

convictions, he would have been the decipherer of Hittite. When his views promptly evoked sharp criticism, however, he retracted his discovery and missed his chance to be the great decipherer for which he was qualified by knowledge and intelligence, but not by disposition.

A discoverer must not allow himself to be discouraged by the critics who are ever present to discredit any major contribution. However stubborn Grotefend may have been (and he was on occasion more stubborn than necessary or desirable), he earned his laurels not only by cracking the Old Persian system but also by retaining his faith in his work. Champollion and Rawlinson ran into their full share of opposition, but they never retracted their decipherments or abandoned their labors. Knudtzon's sterling reputation as an Assyriologist endures, but as a decipherer he was weighed in the scales and found wanting. His lack of self-confidence wiped out his discovery, so that it had to be rediscovered years later by a real pioneer. It is only fair to say, however, that the latter had at his disposal a mass of evidence that was still under the ground in 1902.

Meanwhile fragments of tablets in the same language as the Arzawa letters had been found near Boğazköy by a French explorer, E. Chantre, in 1893. Accordingly, it was clear that whatever the linguistic affinities of the Arzawa letters, they were in the same language of the Hittites used also at Boğazköy, which presumably marked the capital of the Hittite Empire. Sayce realized this and tried to get the British to start excavating there. But Germany had become the main center of cuneiform studies, and the kaiser was interested in the project. Moreover, the German ambassador in Constantinople was influential. So the Germans got the permit to excavate, and they sent the Assyriologist Hugo Winckler to head the expedition in 1905.

After preliminary work in that year, Winckler conducted a major operation at Boğazköy in 1906–8. He uncovered the royal archives, finding more than 10,000 tablets, among them the Akkadian version of the treaty between Hattusilis III and Ramses II long known from the Egyptian version inscribed at Karnak.[5] The style, script, names, and contents of the Boğazköy archives left no doubt as to their historical period. Belonging to the Amarna Age and the Rameside Age that followed it, the Hittite archives came from the fourteenth and thirteenth centuries B.C. They included a great number of tablets in the native Hittite language. In addition to standard Hittite, some of the tablets contained passages in cognate dialects called "Luwian" and "Palaic." Something is known about Luwian, thanks largely to tablets with alternating Hittite and Luwian sections dealing with the same ritual topics.

Moreover, an unrelated language known as Hattic was represented; it was the speech of pre-Hittite inhabitants who had left a deep impression on the Hittite religion so that certain rituals were accompanied by Hattic recitations. Hittite-Hattic bilingual rituals have provided us with some knowledge of Hattic. Akkadian, as the international language, was used extensively. Sumerian as the classical language of the cuneiform world had its place too. Hurrian was also important there. School texts from Hattusas sometimes added Hittite to the Sumerian and Akkadian columns, which eventually helped to teach us some of the details of the Hittite language.

But the main clue to interpreting the Hittite texts was the abundance of ideograms (both Sumerograms and Akkadograms) in the unilinguals. Often the Hittite scribes

5. Note Leo Deuel, *The Treasures of Time* (Cleveland: World Publishing Co., 1961), pp. 256–67, for Winckler's own story.

express the root of a verb or noun ideographically and add the grammatical endings as phonetic complements. This gives us the Hittite inflections, even as the ideograms are a clue to the meaning of the passage. There are also bilinguals and even translations of known literary as well as historic texts. For example, fragments of the Gilgamesh Epic in Hittite (and Hurrian) translation have been found at Boğazköy. There is accordingly no dearth of material for elucidating the Hittite language. But we must not get the idea that the task was easy for the pioneers; like all pioneering work, the first great strides in Hittitology look easy only in retrospect.

A young Assyriologist from Prague had been exposed to the fine school of linguistic science that had grown in his native city. Those were the days before the dissolution of the Austro-Hungarian Empire, and the young scholar Bedřich Hrozný (1879–1952) happened to be teaching in Vienna as the First World War was breaking out. Endowed with the necessary combination of curiosity, originality, brilliance, and daring and equipped with a sound knowledge of cuneiform and linguistics, he embarked on a project to prepare copies of Hittite tablets from Boğazköy for publication. Happily the task provided him with the opportunity of investigating the character and affinities of the Hittite language.

At first some hope was attached to fragments of trilingual dictionaries, in which Sumerian words were rendered in Akkadian and in Hittite in three parallel columns. But such lists contain mostly rare words that are of little use in reading normal texts, and they provide little or none of the grammatical elements. Hrozný therefore worked mainly with unilingual Hittite texts, where the ideograms (both Sumerograms and Akkadograms) provided clues as to the meaning, so that he could make further inferences from context concerning the words and suffixes in true Hittite. The following is one of the key passages interpreted by Hrozný:

nu BREAD-*an e-iz-za-at-te-ni*
wa-a-tar-ma e-ku-ut-te-ni

Hrozný saw that the passage consisted of two parallel halves, which balanced each other, as is clear from the rhyming endings of each half. BREAD is a Sumerogram, whose meaning was already known. Parallel to "bread" is *wa-a-tar*, an Indo-European word cognate with English "water!" Since one eats bread and drinks water, Hrozný was able to infer the meanings of the two verbs. The first is cognate with German *essen*, Latin *edere*, and English *eat*. The suffix -*n* in BREAD-*an* is the accusative case ending (related to -*n* in Greek). A number of other passages showed that *nu* and enclitic -*ma* mean something like "now . . . then . . ." or "both . . . and . . . ." The whole passage is to be translated: "Now bread you eat; water then you drink."

This kind of evidence left no doubt in Hrozný's mind: Hittite was Indo-European. With grammatical inflections and basic vocabulary pointing in the same direction, a real pioneer like Hrozný did not waver. Before he had finished, he had set Hittite on its true course, so that today cuneiform Hittite is one of the best-known languages recovered in the Age of the Decipherments. Moreover, it has exerted a great influence on Indo-European linguistics, for Hittite is the first recorded Indo-European language and is full of interesting phenomena and new evidence.

Hrozný made a detailed study of tablets containing a Hittite law code. The phraseology in such codes was familiar from other cuneiform texts such as Hammurapi's Code, in which the common formula is: "If a person commits such and such an offense, he is to be punished in such and such a way." Accordingly, Hrozný knew the general meaning of sections like the following from the Sumerograms and Akkadograms, and he could attribute the correct sense and grammatical analysis to the Hittite words: *ták-ku* LÚ-ULÙLU EL-LUM QA-AS-SÚ *na-aš-ma* GÌR-ŠU *ku-iš-ki tu-wa-ar-ni-iz-zi nu-uš-še* 20 GÍN KUBABBAR *pa-a-i.* The ideograms (which are in Sumerian or Akkadian or a combination of both) were known to have these meanings: LÚ-ULÙLU, "man"; EL-LUM, "free"; QA-AS-SÚ, "his hand"; GÌR-ŠU, "his foot"; GÍN, "shekel"; and KUBABBAR, "silver." The sense of the entire law is: "If anybody breaks the hand or foot of a free man, he shall pay 20 shekels of silver to him." Note that *ku-iš-ki*, "anybody," is cognate with Latin *quisque. Ták-ku* means "if"; *na-aš-ma*, "or"; *tu-wa-ar-ni-iz-zi*, "breaks"; *nu-uš-še*, "to him"; and *pa-a-i*, "he gives, pays."

On the basis of context, Sumero-Akkadian script and literature, and Indo-European linguistics, Hrozný and his followers have worked out cuneiform Hittite so that we have good grammars, dictionaries, and all the didactic and reference materials that scholars need for mastering the language and interpreting new texts.[6] It should be noted that Hrozný and other cuneiformists were not in a position

6. Johannes Friedrich has supplied the best tools for the study of cuneiform Hittite: *Hethitisches Elementarbuch*, 2 vols. (Heidelberg: Carl Winter, 1940–46); *Hethitisches Wörterbuch* (Heidelberg: Carl Winter, 1952 [with 3 suppls. 1957, 1961, 1966]); and *Hethitisches Keilschrift-Lesebuch* (Heidelberg: Carl Winter, 1960). The standard edition of the Hittite Code is also by Friedrich: *Die hethitischen Gesetze* (Leiden: Brill, 1959). The first fascicle of a new, authoritative lexicon has been published by Hans G. Güterbock and Harry A. Hoffner, *The Hittite Dictionary: of the Oriental Institute of the University of Chicago*, vol. 3, fasc. 1, 1980. (The publication begins with the letter "L" in volume 3 to avoid immediate overlapping with Annlies Kammenhuber's Hittite-German dictionary which will start with "A".)

to integrate Hittite and the other Indo-European languages with linguistic finesse. Professional Indo-Europeanists starting with Ferdinand Sommer rendered this service. And even today, Hittitologists come in two groups—the cuneiformists who take the lead in interpreting the texts, and Indo-Europeanists who deal with linguistic details and bring the evidence of Hittite to bear on comparative Indo-European.

Unlike cuneiform Hittite, which is in a known script, hieroglyphic Hittite had to be deciphered from scratch. We now know that the hieroglyphs express a dialect more closely related to Luwian than to the standard cuneiform Hittite of Hattusas. Royal seals of the Hittite Empire (c. 1400–1200 B.C.) are written in the hieroglyphs, sometimes accompanied by a cuneiform version. Such bilinguals provided opening wedges in the decipherment.

After the collapse of the Empire early in the twelfth century B.C., cuneiform Hittite went out of use. However, city-states on the fringe of the Empire in Syria and Cilicia continued to write Hieroglyphic Hittite, and most of the texts come from those areas and date from the tenth to the end of the eighth centuries B.C., when the spread of Assyrian power put an end to the Hittite tradition in those city-states.

As we have already noted, it was in the early 1870s that Sayce identified the hieroglyphs as Hittite. An unappreciated opening wedge for the decipherment, however, had come to light in 1863, when A.D. Mordtmann published a description of a silver boss (subsequently known to be a regular type of royal Hittite seal) with hieroglyphs and cuneiform writing. The seal, which belonged to a dealer, had previously been offered for sale to the British Museum, where Samuel Birch considered it a copy and

Henry Rawlinson pronounced it a complete fake. Although the Museum did not buy the seal, it made some wax impressions, from which apparently a number of copies have been made.[7] In 1880 Sayce made a careful study of it and rightly concluded that it was a bilingual. For a long time it was known as the Tarkondemos Seal; now it is read:

Tarku-muwa KING *me+r(a)-a* LAND
"Tarkummuwa, King of the Land of Mera"

Sayce correctly identified the ideograms for KING and LAND. From other texts, Sayce isolated the ideograms for CITY ( ) and GOD ( ), as well as the nominative ending (*s*) and the accusative ending (*n*). He did not discover their phonetic values;[8] if he had, he might have realized that the language was Indo-European (compare Greek *anthrōpo-s,* "man," in the nominative with *anthropo-n* in the accusative). Sayce also noted that the ideogram for GOD preceded all divine names and that therefore it served as a determinative.

Around 1890 the French lawyer and Assyriologist Joachim Ménant (1820–99) correctly identified the function of the man pointing to himself ( ) as the pronoun first

7. See #69 (p. 24 and pl. VIII) in C. H. Gordon, "Western Asiatic Seals in the Walters Art Gallery," *Iraq* 6 (1939): 3–34 and pls. II–XV.
8. That is, that the two endings were pronounced *s* and *n*, respectively.

person singular, even as the Egyptian man pointing to himself (𓀀) designates the same pronoun. This was im-

portant because it clarified the style of the Hittite inscriptions that begin "I am So-and-so. . . . "

It was not until the 1930s that four scholars, P. Meriggi, I. Gelb, E. Forrer, and H. Bossert by their cumulative efforts made further progress with the decipherment. Meriggi got the ideogram for "son," which was of use in interpreting the genealogies. Gelb spotted the word "to make" and correctly transliterated it as *aia;* this word helped establish the close affinity of Hieroglyphic Hittite and Luwian. Forrer recognized a formula of imprecation which was of value in delineating sentence structure. Bossert (1889–1962) read the royal name Warpalawa and the name of the goddess Kupapa. The achievement of the 1930s was largely through the establishment of the phonetic values of signs without the aid of bilinguals. This was done by observing that a particular city or land name (whose category was fixed by the CITY or LAND determinative) occurred only in the inscriptions from one particular place. At Carchemish it was assumed that

was to be read

Kar − *ka* − *me* CITY

Sometimes this method was controllable by interlocking syllabic repetitions. For instance, Mar'ash (= *Gur-gu-ma* in Cuneiform Hittite) and Hamath (= *Ḥa-ma-tu* in cuneiform) both have the syllable *ma*. At Gurgumma and Hamath, respectively, the following names could therefore be read thus:

$$Ku+r(a) - ku - ma \quad \text{CITY}$$

and

$$A - ma - tu \quad \text{LAND}$$

At Tuwanuwa (Tyana), the following name could be read with confidence, thanks to the repetition of the syllable *wa* (which is the kind of corroboration found in the repetition of *ku/gu* in Gurgumma). Also, the *tu* ties in with the same sign in *A-ma-tu*, "Hamath":

$$Tu - wa - n(u) - wa \quad \text{CITY}$$

The Assyrian kings mention in their annals the names of several Hittite kings, such as Muwatali of Gurgumma, Urḫilinu of Hamath, and Warpalawa of Tuwanuwa. Accordingly, if inscriptions from such towns or states can be dated to the periods when those kings ruled, it is possible for their personal names to appear in the inscriptions. With this possibility in mind, the search produced the following royal names:

$$Mu - wa - ta - li$$

$$U+r(a) - ḫi - li - n(a)$$

$$Wa+r(a) - pa - la - wa$$

Between 1933 and 1937 more royal seals were found at

Boğazköy, so that scholars learned the hieroglyphic form of the names of most of the great kings. Although most of their names are written ideographically, *Mu-ta-li* (= *Mu-wa-ta-li*) is spelled out syllabically, and the queen's names Puduḫepa and Tanuḫepa are also spelled out and automatically provided the reading of the chief goddess of the Hittite mountain shrine of Yazilikaya:

GOD *Ḫa* — *ba* — *tu* = cuneiform GOD *Ḫe-bat*, "the goddess Ḫebat." (The third sign can be read *ba* or *pa*.)

After the system of the Hittite hieroglyphs had been cracked the hard way by Meriggi, Gelb, Forrer, and Bossert, a great Phoenician and Hieroglyphic Hittite bilingual at Karatepe in Cilicia came to Bossert's attention after the Second World War. A king named Azitawadd had ruled there towards the close of the eighth century B.C. and built a palace embellished with reliefs and inscriptions telling about his accomplishments. The Phoenician text, which is by far the longest known Phoenician inscription, is quite intelligible. Bossert, who happened to be stationed permanently in Turkey, fell heir to the Karatepe finds and, of course, understood the importance of the discovery for the elucidation of Hieroglyphic Hittite.[9] Not being a Semitist, Bossert realized that the best way to proceed was to send copies of the Phoenician text to experts in Northwest Semitic and urge them to publish their translations as promptly as possible. Several, including the present writer,

9. Bossert's own account is reproduced by Ceram, *Hands,* pp. 288–94. For the grammar of hieroglyphic Hittite and its corpus of texts, see Piero Meriggi, *Grammatica,* in *Manuale di Eteo Geroglifico,* vol. 1, and *Testi,* in *Manuale di Eteo Geroglifico,* vol. 2 (Rome: Edizioni dell'-Ateneo, 1966, 1967).

did so and within a short time the Phoenician key to the hieroglyphic version was available. Unfortunately, Bossert did not publish the whole hieroglyphic version; in fact, he released only sections rearranged to match the phraseology of the Phoenician version. And since the Hittite word order is different from the Phoenician, Bossert transposed the Hittite to agree with the Phoenician sequence, so that we could not always know the order of the Hittite words on the original stones. Bossert meanwhile has died, and the full Hittite version of the important text conveniently has been published together with the Phoenician version by Meriggi.[10] But Bossert's articles left no doubt that the Karatepe bilingual would greatly advance our knowledge of hieroglyphic Hittite, particularly in enlarging the vocabulary.

The value of the Karatepe bilingual is enormous, but the first decisive steps in deciphering Hieroglyphic Hittite were made without it. Karatepe confirmed the soundness of the painstaking work done in the 1930s.

The following translation of the Phoenician version will convey an idea of the vocabulary, style, and scope of the Karatepe text:

> I am Azitawadd, the blessed of Baal, the servant of Baal, whom Awarku, King of the Danunites, exalted. Baal made me as a father and a mother to the Danunites. I quickened the Danunites, enlarged the Land of the Plain of Adana, from the rising of the sun to its setting, and in my days the Danunites had every good and plenty and goodness. And I filled the arsenals of Paghar and I multiplied horse upon horse and shield upon shield and camp upon camp by the grace of Baal and the gods. I shattered the insolent (?). And I wiped out all the evil that was in the land. And I erected the house of my lordship in goodness and I did good for the progeny of my lord. And I sat on the throne of his father and made peace with every king. And even

10. Meriggi, *Testi*, pp. 73–89.

(as) in fatherhood (that is, like a father) every king treated me because of my righteousness, wisdom, and goodness of heart. And I built mighty walls in all the outposts on the borders, in places where there had been bad men with gangs, none of whom had been subservient to the House of Mopsh; but I, Azitawadd, put them under my feet and I built settlements in those places for the Danunites to inhabit in the ease of their hearts. And I subjugated mighty lands in the west, which none of the kings before me had subjugated, but I, Azitawadd, subjugated them, bringing them down and settling them in the extremity of my borders in the east, and Danunites I settled there. And there were in my days, in all the borders of the Plain of Adana, from the rising of the sun to its setting—even in places which had formerly been feared, where a man would fear to walk the road, but in my days a woman could stroll with hand on spindles, by the grace of Baal and the gods—yea, there were in all my days plenty and goodness and good living and ease of heart for the Danunites and all the Plain of Adana. And I built this city and made the name Azitawaddiyy because Baal and Reshef-of-the-Stags sent me to build and I built it by the grace of Baal and Reshef-of-the-Stags, in plenty and in goodness and in good living and in ease of heart so that it would be a stronghold for the Plain of Adana and the House of Mopsh. For in my days there were unto the land of the Plain of Adana, plenty and goodness; and in my days it was never night for the Danunites. And I built this city and made the name Azitawaddiyy. I installed Baal K-r-n-t-r-y-sh in (it) and offered a sacrifice for every molten image; a head of large cattle (as) an annual sacrifice, and in the plowing season a head of small cattle, and in the harvest season a head of small cattle. And Baal K-r-n-t-r-y-sh blessed Azitawadd with life and peace and great strength above any other king so that Baal K-r-n-t-r-y-sh and all the deities of the city might give to Azitawadd length of days and multitude of years and good authority (?) and great strength above any other king. And may this city be one of plenty (of food) and wine, and may this people which dwells in it be owners of large and small cattle and owners of plenty (of food) and wine, and procreate (?) very much and be very strong and very obedient to Azitawadd and to the House of Mopsh by the grace of Baal and the gods. And if any king among kings, and prince among princes, or person of renown, who obliterates the name of Azitawadd from this gate and puts (on his own) name, or even covets this city and removes this gate which Azitawadd made, and reuses (it) for a strange gate and puts (his) name on it; whether he removes from covetousness, or from hate and evil he removes this gate; then may Baal of the Heavens and El Creator of Earth, and the Eternal Sun and all the Generation of the Gods obliterate that prince and that king and that man of renown but may the name of Azitawadd endure for ever like the name of the Sun and Moon!

The Phoenicians were an important factor in the Mediterranean throughout the second and first millennia B.C. Their bilinguals written in mixed communities have been of the greatest value in starting, or refining, a number of decipherments. We shall soon see how the Phoenician version of a Cypriot bilingual provided the key to the Cypriot syllabary. In the summer of 1964 inscriptions on gold were found in Phoenician and Etruscan at Pyrgi, on the Italian coast about thirty miles northwest of Rome. The Pyrgi find is a valuable asset in furthering the decipherment of Etruscan, though the unknown affinities of that language have so far prevented the specialists from ascertaining as much as we would like to know about its grammar and vocabulary. Etruscan is written in a form of the familiar alphabet, so that there is no difficulty concerning the pronunciation. The symbiosis of Phoenicians and Etruscans in Italy early in the fifth century B.C. is in itself interesting. It now appears that the Phoenicians were at an early date on Italian soil, where they could exert direct influence not only on the Etruscans (who, in turn, contributed so much to Roman culture) but for that matter on the Romans themselves.[11]

---

11. The partial recovery of the Etruscan language is described by Johannes Friedrich, *Extinct Languages* (New York: Philosophical Library, 1957), pp. 137–43; Doblhofer, *Voices*, pp. 295–301; and Cleator, *Lost Languages* pp. 167–69.

6

UGARITIC:
DECIPHERMENT
AND IMPACT

All the decipherments we have considered so far have dealt with inscriptions that had been available for some time before they could be read. Some of the breakthroughs were achieved quickly, but the process of attaining a fairly complete decipherment was spread over decades. Ugaritic does not follow this pattern. The texts, in a totally new script, were first found in 1929; the decipherment was effected in 1930.

Ugaritic literature is important in the history of Western

civilization. It has revolutionized Old Testament studies and also bridged the gap between Homer and the Bible.[1] In content, Ugaritic is the foremost literary discovery made so far in the twentieth century.[2] Its impact eventually will be felt at all levels of teaching the origins of our culture, although, as is often the case, the elementary and secondary textbooks used in our schools lag as much as half a century behind the discovery and decipherment.

Ugarit had been completely blotted out of human memory. Its name first reappeared in the Amarna tablets. The rediscovery of its site, which the Arabs now call Ras esh-Shamra (Fennel Head), was accidental. In 1928 a Syrian peasant, plowing in a field between the mound of Ugarit and the nearby Mediterranean shore, struck a stone slab. It was part of a tomb that archaeologists describe as Mycenaean. Since the area is Semitic and Ugarit is located in Northern Phoenicia, the Mycenaean structure foreshadowed discoveries linking the Phoenicians and the Aegean around 1400–1200 B.C. in the latter half of the Late Bronze Age.

In 1929 excavations at Ugarit were begun by the French, who were then governing Syria. The diggers, under the direction of Claude Schaeffer and Georges Chenet, soon found cuneiform tablets, some in Akkadian and others in a new script. The tablets were turned over to an eminent Assyriologist, Charles Virolleaud (1879–1968), for publication. He issued the first forty-eight tablets in the new Ugaritic script in the journal *Syria*, dated 1929: the same year in which they were found.

---

1. C. H. Gordon, *The Common Background of Greek and Hebrew Civilizations* (New York: Norton, 1965).

2. The literary tablets are translated by C. H. Gordon, "Poetic Legends and Myths from Ugarit," *Berytus* 25 (1977): 5–133.

The progress of Ugaritic studies is due largely to Virolleaud's character and ability. He prepared the source material promptly for publication. In four decades of pioneering and making basic contributions to Ugaritic, Professor Virolleaud was never responsible for delays in placing new material in the hands of international Orientalists. He was very generous towards other workers in the subject. To cite only one instance, he gave his transliteration of an unpublished literary text to the present writer to be included in the latter's *Ugaritic Handbook*. This kind of generosity is not common. Virolleaud, in addition to his learning, was endowed with a keen eye and a fine hand for draftsmanship, so that his copies are models of accuracy and clarity.

In his 1929 article,[3] Virolleaud laid the foundations for the decipherment not only through making source material available to everyone but also through some sound observations. He perceived that the script runs from left to right, that the small number of signs (not over thirty) can only represent an alphabet, that a little vertical wedge serves to separate the words, and that the shortness of the words (often represented by only one or two letters) means that none or few of the vowels are indicated in the script.

A group of six signs appeared on some bronze adzes:

(which we now can read: *rb khnm*, "the High Priest"). On tablet 18, which has the same format as Akkadian epistles, Virolleaud noted that this group of signs was preceded by a one-letter word

3. Charles Virolleaud, "Les inscriptions cunéiformes de Ras Shamra," *Syria* 10 (1929): 304–10 and pls. LXI–LXXX.

(which we can now read *l . rb . khnm*). From the epistolary

style of Mesopotamia, Virolleaud concluded that 𝕐𝕐𝕐 is a

uniconsonantal word meaning "to" (for the epistles regularly begin "To So-and-so"). Virolleaud was right, and although he did not identify the Ugaritic language or assign
any phonetic values to the signs, he succeeded in isolating
a word and gave it its correct meaning.

A German Semitist, Hans Bauer (1878–1937), soon applied
himself to the decipherment of Ugaritic and got positive
results quickly.[4] He had been a cryptanalyst in the First
World War and also had learned some of the basic problems
concerning the decipherment of forgotten scripts by working on the Sinaitic inscriptions. Bauer's success was the
result of a fundamental assumption: he sensed that the
language was Semitic because the words, separated by dividers, are short—a characteristic of the Semitic languages
as contrasted with the Indo-European and many other
families. Moreover, Syria had long been populated by
Northwest Semites such as the Phoenicians, Hebrews,
Arameans, and other closely related Northwest Semites.
This being the case, the uniconsonantal word for "to" had
to be *l*, because *la* means "to" in all the Northwest Semitic
languages.

As a seasoned expert on Semitic grammar, Bauer knew
that in Northwest Semitic some letters are common as
prefixes and some as suffixes. It happens that *t* and *n* are
letters of fairly high frequency that serve as both prefixes

4. Ugarit and the decipherment of its script are discussed by Leo Deuel,
Testaments of Time (New York: Alfred A. Knopf, 1965), pp. 224–53; Ernst Doblhofer
Voices in Stone (New York: Viking Press, 1961), pp. 203–20; P.E. Cleator, *Lost Languages* (New York: John Day, 1959), pp. 135–44; and Alan D. Corré, "Anatomy of
a Decipherment," *Wisconsin Academy of Sciences, Arts and Letters* 55 (1966): 11–20.

and suffixes. He found two Ugaritic letters, which we shall call X and Z, that satisfied all the requirements of frequency and position for *n* and *t*, but he could not yet tell which was which. He then noted a list of what looked like personal names, each consisting of three words always with the same two-letter word (for which we shall substitute the symbols "YZ") in the middle. Since Semitic names follow the pattern "A son of B," Bauer read YZ as *bn*, "son." This produced the values Y = *b*, Z = *n*, and (by the process of elimination) X = *t*. Since *b* is often prefixed to words, it fitted well for the Northwest Semitic prefix *b* "in." Now Bauer could seek the name of the popular Canaanite god *b*ᶜ*l*, "Baal," for he knew both *b* and *l*. He spotted *b*W*l* and concluded that W = ᶜ. There was now no trouble in reading *b*ᶜ*lt*, "Baalat" (the feminine of "Baal"), for all the letters had been identified.

In a series of words that looked like numerals, Bauer saw that QlQ had to be "3," written *tlt* in Arabic. Pattern alone would have sufficed for this identification because there is no other familiar root in Semitic texts with the same consonant at the beginning and end and with *l* in the middle. Another numeral, RSbᶜ, could only be *arbᶜ*, yielding two more values. Now the group ᶜ*ttrt* could be read as the name of the goddess Astarte, for all the letters were known. The numeral *a*U*t* could only be the feminine *aḫt* "one"; so that the similar numeral *aḫ*V had to be the masculine *aḫd* "one."[5]

The decipherment of Ugaritic was essentially a problem of mono-alphabetic substitution. It was complicated, however, by the presence of three aleph signs (*'a*, *'i*, *'u*), differing according to the vocalization. Also, there are two homo-

---

5. The logic in this reasoning presupposes a knowledge of Hebrew.

phonous signs for *s*. Rather brilliantly, Bauer saw that *XlYZ*, standing parallel to *b^cl*, was *'ilh-*, "god." He was wrong about the final letter Z but right about X and Y, thus discovering another aleph (which we now transliterate *'i*) as well as the *h*. He was bothered by the fact that more than one aleph had been revealed through his decipherment, but like a true discoverer he did not let himself get bogged down in doubts; instead, he confidently declared that this "fact" must prepare us for further examples of homophony. Actually, the only instance of homophony in the Ugaritic alphabet is the pair of *s* signs. The alephs are differentiated by the vowels they carry. But Bauer's positive and confident approach made his achievement possible. The kind of perfectionism that makes of every unsolved detail an insurmountable barrier precludes any kind of pioneering work.

Some of Bauer's mistakes were corrected by a French orientalist, Édouard Dhorme (1881–1966), who was not only an able Old Testament scholar and cuneiformist but also had been decorated by the French government for his cryptanalytic services in the First World War. Dhorme helped to refine the decipherment not only by correcting Bauer but also by adding the phonetic values of still other letters in 1930. Meanwhile, Virolleaud was working on the decipherment, too. As far as priority in print goes, Bauer published first.[6] Bauer should not be criticized for rushing into

6. He received the issue of *Syria* with Virolleaud's texts and comments on 22 April 1930, identified enough of the letters to get the decipherment started by 27 April, informed René Dussaud of his success on 28 April, and sent his preliminary report to the *Vossische Zeitung* on 15 May. On 4 June 1930 the *Vossische Zeitung* printed his article, in which he claimed to have read at least twenty letters correctly (though, in fact only seventeen were right). With the help of Dhorme's corrections and improvements, Bauer wrote up the decipherment of Ugaritic in keeping with what he called his "Alphabet of October 5, 1930" in a book called *Entzifferung der Keilschrifttafeln von Ras Schamra* (Halle/Salle: Max Niemeyer Ver-

print in a newspaper instead of biding his time to appear in a dignified, scientific journal. Such criticism would fail to reckon with a basic characteristic of decipherers: they not only want credit for their accomplishment, but they want to come in first. Second or third place gives small satisfaction to a man with the spirit of a champion.

Virolleaud went beyond Bauer and Dhorme in 1930. In that year more tablets were unearthed, including major literary compositions that were turned over to Virolleaud for publication. Virolleaud's role in the decipherment of Ugaritic may therefore be compared in some ways to Rawlinson's in the decipherment of the Achaemenian inscriptions. Both of these scholars went further than their fellow decipherers because of constant work on a larger corpus of material than was at the disposal of anyone else. We pay our tribute to Bauer, who published his decipherment first (4 June 1930) and to Dhorme, who improved on Bauer's initial work in an article that came off press about 1 October 1930. But Virolleaud is the father of Ugaritology for much the same reasons that Rawlinson is the father of Assyriology. On 3 October 1930 Virolleaud's results were announced in Paris at a session of the Académie des Inscriptions et Belles-Lettres. On the twenty-fourth of that month, he addressed the Académie on his methods and on the contents of the newly discovered literary texts. That address, with some revision, forms the basis of his article on the decipherment of Ugaritic in the 1931 volume of *Syria*, in which he came close to achieving the right values for

lag, 1930). The introduction on pp. 1–16 is a masterpiece of decipherment description. Bauer gives a more refined account in *Das Alphabet von Ras Schamra* (Halle/-Salle: Max Niemeyer Verlag, 1932). Dhorme's "Le déchiffrement des tablettes de Ras Schamra" has been reprinted in *Recueil Édouard Dhorme* (Paris: Imprimerie Nationale, 1951), pp. 531–36, 767.

nearly all of the signs in the alphabet.[7] To Virolleaud we owe the first edition and pioneer interpretation of nearly all the Ugaritic tablets, except the relatively few published by others after his death. His publications since 1929 are coextensive with the history of the subject, from mysterious beginnings to the establishment of Ugaritic as a major Semitic language taught today in scores of universities and seminaries the world over.

The present writer's involvement in Ugaritic began in 1935, after the decipherment was a *fait accompli*. It is only natural that during the 1930s the exciting nature of the Ugaritic tablets should have captured the imagination of many scholars with varying degrees of linguistic preparation. The result was a huge output of literature, in which the student was often unable to separate the wheat from the chaff. Moreover, the burgeoning crop of new scholars interested in the field needed a textbook with a detailed formulation of rules. My *Ugaritic Grammar*, published in 1940, attempted to meet this need. The discovery of new texts and the contributions of many scholars, however, kept raising the general level of the field, so that enlarged revisions of the work appeared; the most recent, *Ugaritic Textbook*, contains not only a grammar but a dictionary, a corpus of texts in transliteration, cuneiform reading selections, and other features designed, as the case may be, for the beginner or for the advanced scholar.[8]

Bilinguals turned up too late to contribute anything to the decipherment. One such text is quite interesting. It lists the Ugaritic alphabet and provides the pronunciation of

---

7. Charles Virolleaud, "Le déchiffrement des tablettes alphabétiques de Ras-Shamra," *Syria* 12 (1931): 15–23.

8. Published by the Pontifical Biblical Institute in Rome. The book appeared in 1965; it was reprinted with a supplement in 1967.

each letter in terms of Akkadian signs. Had this tablet been found in 1929, it would have served as the key to the decipherment. But it was discovered in 1955, a quarter of a century too late to be of any use.

The importance of Ugaritic transcends its decipherment interest and its technical value in Semitic linguistics. Its literature occupies a major link in the chain of Western civilization. This is hinted in a type of school text, several copies of which have been unearthed; they are quite little tablets containing the ABC of thirty letters already arranged in the fixed traditional order inherited by the Hebrews, Greeks, and Romans. The Ugaritic sequence of letters has, in spite of the accidents of transmission, come down to us in the familiar order as regards the following letters: *a b — d — — — — h i/j k l m n o p q r s t u/v — — — —*. A study of Ugaritic literature in its Mediterranean setting shows that we have inherited more than just the alphabet from the sphere to which Ugarit belonged.

It was recognized from the start of the decipherment that Ugaritic was closely related to Hebrew and Phoenician. Soon whole expressions emerged, closely paralleling Old Testament expressions. To take only one of many:

⟨ⁿUgaritic cuneiform⟩	מטל השמים
⟨ⁿUgaritic cuneiform⟩	ומשמני הארץ
ṭl • šmm •	*m-ṭl h-šmym*
šmn • arṣ	*w-m-šmny h-arṣ*
Dew of heavens	From the dew of the heavens
Fat of Earth	And from the fat of the earth

Note that the vocabulary is quite similar; the consonantal skeleton is the same in Hebrew and Ugaritic for "dew" (*ṭl*), "heavens" (*šmm*), "fat" (*šmn*), and "earth" (*arṣ*). Moreover, the poetic parallelism is identical. Instead of rhyme and meter, we find the poetic unit characterized by balanced members: "dew of heavens" is balanced by "fat of earth," for both are manifestations of fertility in the same tradition.

Hundreds of Ugaritic parallels to the Hebrew Bible have revolutionized the study of the Old Testament. The Old Testament scholars took this in their stride. Their field had weathered the storm of *Babel und Bibel,* and they were used to newly discovered Semitic texts bearing on Hebrew Scripture. It was soon evident that the Hebrews had not invented their language or literary forms; they had inherited them from the older Canaanite population. It was the content rather than the form of the Old Testament that embodied the original Hebrew contribution. Scripture forbids the Chosen People to commit the abominations of the old native population. Some of the abominations—like copulating with animals—are now attested not only in the Bible, which might be considered biased against the Canaanites, but also in the Ugaritic religious texts, where it has a sacred and honored place in the Baal cult.[9] A few Ugaritic texts have been found in Palestine: at Beth-Shemesh, Taanach, and Mount Tabor. There can be little doubt that the kind of literary texts found at Ugarit also circulated in Palestine before the Hebrew conquest.[10]

The Ugaritic Epic of Kret deals with a hero who established his royal line through children whose birth was promised by the gods. The same feature appears in the only

---

9. Leviticus 18:23–30; Ugaritic text 67:V:17–22.

10. The Ugaritic Epic of Aqhat and Danel is referred to in Ezekiel 14:14 and 27:3; see C. H. Gordon, *Ugarit and Minoan Crete* (New York: Norton, 1966), p. 25. That the story was at home in Israel since the second millennium is suggested by the fact that Levi's son Qhat (English "Kohath") is named after Aqhat, while the Hebrew midwife Pu^cah (Exodus 1:15) is named after Pughat, Aqhat's sister (Ugaritic *pûghat* can only correspond to Hebrew *pu^cah* by phonetic law).

other epic found at Ugarit so far, the Epic of Aqhat, in which a virtuous ruler is blessed with a son through divine favor. This is of a piece with the Genesis stories of the Patriarchs, who founded a royal line through the intervention of God. This is especially clear in the birth of Isaac to Sarah and Abraham.

The Epic of Kret deals also with the recapture by King Kret of his destined bride, Hurrai, from the distant fortress of another king. This is the Helen of Troy motif. What emerged is that in Mycenaean times (in which the epics of Ugarit, the biblical Patriarchs, and the Trojan War are rooted) all the epics deal with royalty and highlight the recapture of the destined bride, for also in Genesis we read that twice Abraham had to get back his wife Sarah from the harems of other kings.[11]

Ugarit shows that however different classical Greece was from classical Israel, both were rooted culturally in the same Heroic Age during the the latter half of the second millennium B.C.

---

11. All these factors are discussed with documentation in Gordon, *Common Background.*

7

THE AEGEAN
SYLLABARY

The earliest inscriptions writ-
ten on European soil are from Crete and are generally
called "Minoan." The script started out as pictographic and
is sometimes called "Cretan Hieroglyphs." But the most
pictorial inscription that has been found so far is the quite
distinctive Phaistos Disk, written spirally and composed by
impressing dies in the clay when it was still soft. More
cursive forms of the script were developed for common use.

The Minoan system of writing was used for at least two quite different languages: Minoan and Mycenaean. The Minoan texts are called Linear A and the Mycenaean tablets Linear B, following the terminology established by Arthur Evans, who first found both categories of text at Knossos. However, the system of writing spread outside Crete to other areas of the East Mediterranean. Mycenaean tablets have been found in peninsular Greece, notably at Pylos and Mycenae. An offshoot of the system has been discovered by Porphyrios Dikaios at Enkomi, Cyprus, from the Late Bronze Age. The system of writing is a syllabary where each sign represents a consonant followed by a vowel. Apart from the economic and administrative texts in Linear A and B, which we shall discuss later, the system is purely phonetic and avoids ideograms and determinatives. The only non-phonetic sign is the word divider, a great help in any decipherment. The system was so strongly entrenched in East Mediterranean culture that it survived in Crete, and especially in Cyprus, until the Hellenistic Age, when it was used in addition to the alphabet.

Around the middle of the nineteenth century, the Duc de Luynes[1] chanced upon some Cypriot syllabic texts and called them to the attention of scholars in Europe in 1852. But it was not until the discovery of a bilingual Phoenician-Cypriot inscription in 1869 that there was a basis for an inspired pioneer to decipher the Cypriot syllabary. The Phoenician text (published by R. H. Lang in 1872) is not intact, but nearly all of it can be restored from other inscriptions of the same monarch, King Milkiyaton of Idalion and Kition. The restored Phoenician text, in transliteration, runs thus:

1. Honoré Théodore Paul Joseph d'Albert (1802–67).

[*bymm ? lyrḥ ?*] *bšnt 'rb^c 4 lmlk mlkytn* [*mlk*]
[*kty w'dyl sml*]*'z 'š ytn wyṭn'* · *'dnn* · *b^clr*[*m*]
[*bn^cbdmlk l'l*]*y lršp mkl* · *k šm^c qly brk*
[On the day ? of the month ?] in the year four 4 of the reign
of Milkiyaton, [King]
[of Kition and Idalion.] This is [the statue] that our Lord Baal-
ro[m]
[the son of Abdimilk] gave and set up [for] his [god] Reshef-
Mukl, because he heard his voice (and) blessed.

The Cypriot version can now be rendered as follows:[2]

[*i to-i* · *te-ta-ra-to-i* · *we-te-i*] · *pa-si-le-wo-se* ·
   mi-li-ki-ya-to-no-se · *ke-ti-o-ne* · *ka-e-ta-li-o-ne* ·
   pa-si-le-u-
[*o-to-se* · *ta-ne e-pa-ko-*]*me-na-ne* · *to pe-pa-me-ro-ne*
   · *ne-wo-so-ta-ta-se* · *to-na-ti-ri-ya-ta-ne* · *to-te*
   ka-te-se-ta-se · *o wa-na-xe*
[*pa-a-la-ro-mo-se* ·] *o a-pi-ti-mi-li-ko-ne* · *to a-po-lo-ni* ·
   to a-mu-ko-lo-i · *a-po-i wo-i* · *ta-se* · *e-u-ko-la-se*
[*e*]-*pe-tu-ke* · *i tu-ka-i* · *a-za-ta-i*
[In the fourth year] when King Milkiyaton was rul[ing] Kition
and Idalion on the last [of the] five [inter]calary days, Prince
[Baalrom] the [son] of Abdimilk erected this statue for Apollo
of Amyklai, from whom he had obtained for himself [his]
desires. In good luck!

The direction of the writing in both halves of this bilingual is from right to left, as is evident from the fact that in
the last line of each, the unused extra space is on the left.

It was George Smith, the Assyriologist, who deciphered
Cypriot writing in 1872 on the basis of this bilingual. First,
he correctly assumed from the large number of signs (about
fifty-five) that the script is a syllabary; no alphabet has that
many letters.

2. The transliteration makes it easier for the reader to follow, but the decipherer, of course, did not know the pronunciation of any of the signs when he
began the study of the text.

On seeking the Cypriot rendition of the cluster of three names that appear in Phoenician as *Mlkytn* (Milkiyaton), *Kty* (Kition), and *'dyl* (Idalion), Smith noted that the syllable which we now know to be *li* occurs in the first and third names, now read *mi-li-ki-ya-to-no-se* and *e-ta-li-o-ne*. The identification of the names supplied phonetic values. Matching up the name of Idalion with *X-Y-li-*, we obtain $X = i$ (which we now prefer to transliterate as *e*) and $Y = da$ (actually this sign stands for either *ta* or *da*, and it is now conventional to write *ta*, though *da* is no less correct). The first syllable of the king's name has to be *mi-*, because the *m* is fixed by the Phoenician and the *i* is what indicated the use of the *li* sign to represent vowelless *l*. The royal name also yields *ya*, *to*, and *no*. Smith further observed that *mlk*, which can stand for either the verb "to rule" or the noun "king," occurs twice. This corresponded to the repetition inherent in *pa-si-le-wo-se* and *pa-si-le-u-*[ ]. Smith wrongly assumed that *mlk* is "king" in the genitive on the first occasion but nominative in the second and that the same holds for the Greek. There are a number of errors in this assumption, but it happens that the first of the two occurrences in the Greek is indeed the genitive of "king." Then Smith asked himself, "In what known language is the penultimate syllable different in the nominative and genitive of the word for king?" He decided on Greek, in which the nominative for "king" is *basileus* but the genitive is *basilēos*. In spite of flaws in his analysis, Smith came up with the right identification of the language—Greek; and he correctly identified *ba* (we now prefer *pa*, but *ba* is no less correct because the sign covers *pa* and *ba*), *si*, and *le*.

The few foregoing conclusions and identifications cracked the system so that further progress could be made. Thus, the Phoenician name *'bdmlk* could be matched with the name that we now transliterate *a-pi-ti-mi-li-ko-ne* through the identification of *mi-li* (known from Milkiya-ton's name).

Smith established eighteen values with a high degree of probability and proceeded to read Greek names in various Cypriot inscriptions with a fair degree of accuracy. His limited knowledge of Greek prevented him from refining his decipherment. His work was carried on by men with training in classical Greek; first by the Egyptologist Samuel Birch (1813–85), who had assisted Smith, and then by the German numismatist Johannes Brandis (1830–73). The finishing touches were made by a succession of Hellenists, and now we have specialists in Cypriot Greek inscriptions such as T. B. Mitford and Olivier Masson. The standard edition of the texts is Masson's *Les inscriptions Chypriotes syllabiques.*[3]

Smith's achievement illustrates a number of phenomena that recur in the annals of the decipherments. Through seeking he discovered truth even though his premises were not entirely correct. He also established the language (as Greek) on the basis of a single word ("king"). A pioneer has to start somewhere, and if he makes a sweeping generalization on the basis of a single word, this is part of the method of the decipherer. Meticulous philologians who cannot get themselves to make a broad inference without a vast array of supporting evidence will never decipher a forgotten script nor reconstruct a forgotten language. A decipherer must guess, but he must have the sense to know when his guesses are wrong, for they will often be wrong, in which case he must discard them. It is the lucky guess that pays off. When the lucky guess leads to the breakthrough, the

---

3. (Paris: Boccard, 1961). See p. 246 for the bilingual used by Smith to solve the syllabary.

decipherer experiences an illumination comparable to the illumination that mystics know. But the breakthrough must be objectively demonstrable if it is to be accepted as a reality instead of a mirage.

The inscriptions of Cyprus down into the Hellenistic Age are in two languages, Phoenician and Greek. The Greek texts are written sometimes in Greek letters and sometimes in the Cypriot syllabary. The Phoenician alphabet is, of course, used for Phoenician inscriptions. There are also non-Greek inscriptions written in the syllabary, and it is no wonder that a few scholars have suspected that the Eteocypriot inscriptions (as the non-Greek syllabic texts from Cyprus are called) contemporary with the Greek Cypriot syllabic inscriptions are Phoenician. The population may well have used more than two languages, but we know that the main two were Greek and Phoenician. A scholar named A. Mentz tried his hand at interpreting the Eteocypriot version of a bilingual as Semitic, but his readings are wrong. This does not mean that his premise is wrong. Just as we have noted that correct facts sometimes emerge from wrong premises, a correct hunch may be backed up with completely mistaken support, so that the hunch is discredited. Obviously, scholarship cannot treat unproved (though possibly correct) guesses on the same plane as proven fact. The reason Mentz could not get correct readings in the Eteocypriot was not that he lacked perspective, intuition, or intelligence but simply that he did not know enough Semitics or cryptanalysis. The problem must therefore be tackled afresh.

An Amathus bilingual in Eteocypriot and Attic Greek of the fourth century B.C. reads thus:

(Eteocypriot) *a-na* · *ma-to-ri* · *u-mi-e-s[a]-i mu-ku-la-i la-sa-na*
· *a-ri-si-to-no-se a-ra-to-wa-na-ka-so-ko-o-se*
ke-ra-ke-re-tu-lo-se · *ta-ka-na-[?-?]-so-ti* · *a-lo* ·
ka-i-li-po-ti

(Greek) *hē polis hē amathousiōna Aristōna Aristōnaktos eupatridēn*

This bilingual proves that the signs in Eteocypriot texts have the same values as in the Cypriot Greek texts, for *a-ri-si-to-no-se* represents the personal name Ariston mentioned in the Greek. The same holds for the name of Ariston's father, Aristonax, although the Eteocypriot uses the dialectal variant Artowanax (*a-ra-to-wa-na-ka-so-*). Following a Semitic usage, personal names can be accompanied by demonstrative pronouns. These pronouns may be suffixed and prefixed simultaneously: *sa-na a-ri-si-to-no-se* "this Ariston" (literally, "this Ariston-this").

The Greek version is quite clear: "The city of the Amathusans (honored) the noble Ariston (son) of Aristonax." The verb is omitted as often in such dedicatory inscriptions. But we have an idea of how the people of Amathus honored Ariston. The text is written on a stone with footmarks for holding a statue. The erection of Ariston's statue was accordingly the honor awarded him.

The clearest correspondence between the two versions is at the opening of the text: the first two words in the Greek are "the" and "city"; the same holds for the Eteocypriot: *a-na* (or *hâna*), "the, this" in various West Semitic languages, and *ma-to-ri* (pronounced *madōr* + *ē*) "habitation(s), city." Both versions therefore start with "the city." Since the city did something "for" Ariston, the Semitic preposition *la*, "for," is appropriate in *la-sa-na* · *a-ri-si-to-*

no-se "for this Ariston." The details are discussed in my *Evidence for the Minoan Language.*[4]

The fact that both the West Semites and the Greeks used the old syllabary into Hellenistic times, long after the introduction and spread of the alphabet, reflects the deep roots of the syllabary in Cypriot culture. It has therefore occurred to scholars that there may be a connection between the Cypro-Minoan tablets found by Porphyrios Dikaios at Enkomi of the Late Bronze Age (shortly before 1200 B.C.) and Eteocypriot. Some of the signs look alike in both systems, but other signs do not. Since over half a millennium separates the Enkomi tablets from the Eteocypriot texts, considerable changes in form would in any case be expected. Inasmuch as the trend in Cyprus between the Late Bronze Age and the Hellenistic period was the growth of the Greek population and the simultaneous diminution of the West Semites, it seems more likely that the Enkomi texts are Semitic than Greek. But there are other possibilities. Hurrian has been suggested.

The Aegean had been the home of a syllabary since the Middle Bronze Age. We need not delve here into its origins. In a world acquainted with various systems of writing, including Sumero-Akkadian Cuneiform and Hieroglyphic Egyptian, new scripts were bound to appear by the process of stimulus diffusion. The genetic relationship between the Cretan syllabary of the Middle Bronze Age and the Cypriot syllabary of the seventh to third centuries B.C. should have been obvious from the start. In retrospect, we know that seven of the signs are the same in form and

---

4. (Ventnor, N.J.: Ventnor Publishers, 1966), pp. 5–7. The unexplained elements in the Eteocypriot version of the Amathus bilingual are considerable and impose caution on us. For example, the method of indicating the patronymic (son of) remains enigmatic.

sound, in both sets of texts. And yet the dissimilarity of other signs (mostly owing to chronological and local differences) was enough to prevent the decipherment of the older Cretan syllabary on the basis of the later Cypriot sign forms.

The man who unearthed Minoan civilization was Arthur Evans (1851–1941). Like Heinrich Schliemann, whose faith in the Homeric text had led him to the buried cities of the Mycenaeans, Evans attached weight to the ancient traditions about the greatness of Knossos and of Minoan civilization on Crete. Evans could not accept the common opinion that the splendid culture of the Heroic Age around the Aegean was illiterate. The first step towards his discovery of the Minoan and Mycenaean tablets was his tracking down a group of seal stones that peasants were finding on Crete. They bear signs that are often called Cretan hieroglyphs, dating from the early part of the second millennium B.C. Evans was interested in all of Minoan Crete, but he concentrated his efforts on the excavation of the chief center, Knossos, where he found tablets which could be divided into two main categories that he called Linear A and Linear B. The Linear B tablets are far more numerous, but on Crete they are still limited to Knossos. The Linear A texts, though fewer in number, are found on stone and metal as well as on clay at many sites throughout Crete.

Evans noted on a Linear B tablet a word of two signs that looked like *po-lo* in the Cypriot syllabary. Since the word was followed by the MANELESS HORSE determinative, Evans compared *po-lo* with Greek *pōlos*, "foal" (cognate with English "foal"). Now we know that his reading is right. Had Evans stuck to it, he would have initiated the decipherment of Linear B, but he rejected it as a coincidence because it did not agree with his theory that Linear B was Minoan and non-Greek. Any scholar who cannot shake off a false theory is not destined to become a decipherer. However, Evans knew from the rather pictorial signs on the B tablets the objects they dealt with: grain, animals, personnel, clothing, ceramic and metal vessels, chariots, weapons, and so forth. Such signs serving as ideograms or determinatives can be distinguished from the phonetic signs of the syllabary. The numerals, which follow a decimal system, were also clear to Evans.

Many writers made stabs at reading the tablets; one scholar, A. E. Cowley, suggested that two words (which we now read *ko-wo* and *ko-wa*) might be the Greek words *kouros*, "boy," and *kourē*, "girl," though he confused the genders. Cowley certainly did not anticipate the phonetic discrepancy between the Mycenaean and classical Greek forms of these words, nor did he have any inkling that the second syllable would embody *w* instead of *r*. But it is remarkable that Cowley implied the correct Greek identification of the Linear B tablets, and he did identify a pair of words with the correct Greek pair. But his insight led nowhere because he lacked the measure of dedication to the problem necessary to offset the false non-Greek hypothesis of Evans, who had many followers.

Interest in the decipherment of Linear A and B was widespread because the scripts recorded the earliest historically important documents composed on European soil and were bound to shed light on the emergence of the Greeks in the Bronze Age.[5] It was sensed that the tablets

---

5. The earliest known European texts are three little unintelligible clay tablets excavated at Tartaria, in Rumanian Transylvania, from the early part of the third millennium B.C. (c. 2700 B.C., according to carbon 14 tests). They are proof of early literacy around the Balkans and suggest connections with Sumer. But beyond this it is hard to evaluate them historically and, at present, they cannot be compared in importance with the Minoan inscriptions.

would somehow be associated with the Heroic Age, when Achaeans and Trojans fought the war that inspired the *Iliad*. Evans has an immortal name among the pioneers in archaeological discovery. That he revealed Minoan civilization, even as Schliemann had unearthed Mycenaean civilization, is an outstanding accomplishment that can never be taken away from him. But he also hoped to become the decipherer of Minoan, a task for which he was unsuited. His natural intelligence led him to differentiate sharply between Linear A and B, but his theory that the non-Greek Minoans were the only heroes in the act forced him to identify the languages of the two distinct categories of tablet. The Linear B tablets, as distinct from the Linear A, turned out to be quite Greek. In 1939, when Carl Blegen found many Linear B tablets at Pylos, it became clear that the B tablets at Knossos reflected the conquest of that city by mainlanders. (Later the excavation of more B tablets at Mycenae and elsewhere confirmed this.) But Evans would not face the implications of any evidence that ran counter to his pet theory.

To make sure that no one else anticipated him in the decipherment, Evans withheld the publication of most of the Knossos tablets. Accordingly, his death in 1941 was a necessary prelude to progress. Meanwhile, the war years provided cryptanalytic training for a number of the scholars destined to contribute to the decipherment of Linear A and B. It was a foregone conclusion that the task should start with the abundant B tablets instead of the relatively few A tablets. The addition of the newly discovered mainland texts to the thousands of Knossos texts, now released for publication, gave a new impetus to the challenge of decipherment.

Alice Kober of Brooklyn College performed sound and

methodical work on the analysis of the B tablets between 1943 and her premature death in 1950. She did not assign phonetic values or try to pronounce any of the words, let alone identify the language. But methodologically her work was outstanding, and at the time of her death the lines along which she was working were superior to anyone else's. She noted sets of words following the pattern XYZA, XYZB, and XYC and reasoned that the language was inflected with suffixes something like Latin:

a-mi-cu-s
a-mi-cu-m
a-mi-ci

In a syllabary of the Cypriot type, this would mean that the word had three consonants in the stem and that C started with the same consonant as Z but ended in a different vowel.

She noted that there were several such "triplets" of the above type. We shall represent a second set thus: QRSA, QRSB, and QRD. The A and B here are the same signs as the A and B in XYZA and XYZB above. For reasons given above, D in QRD reflects the same third consonant that we find in the stem QRS. Kober deduced that C (in XYC) and D (in QRD), though starting with different consonants, ended in the same vowel, on the correct assumption that they illustrated the same inflection:

XYZA : : QRSA (compare *a-mi-cu-s*)
XYZB : : QRSB (compare *a-mi-cu-m*)
XYC : : QRD (compare *a-mi-ci*)

She, of course, did not imply that the endings were those of Latin *amicus* nor that the language was Latin but only that we are confronted with a language of an inflected type, in which the conjugations and declensions required the variation of the final vowel, the addition of a consonant to the stem, or both.

The method of aligning parallel sets of inflected forms made it possible to chart the signs so that those beginning with the same consonant were on the same horizontal row, while those ending in the same vowel would appear in the same vertical column. Such a chart is sometimes called a "grid," and the method of establishing it is called the "grid system." If we were starting to make a grid on the basis of the above two examples, signs Z and C would appear on the same horizontal row, while signs S and D would appear on another horizontal row, but C and D would be in the same vertical column.

Kober assembled a number of such triplets, including the following in parallel contexts, in the same or similar tablets. The first form modifies the names of women (categorized by the WOMAN determinative); the second form modifies the names of men (categorized by the MAN determinative):

	I	II	III	IV	V	VI	VII	VIII
Form 1:	JKLA	MNLA	OPQA	RSQA	TUVQA	PBWA	XYA	HIA
Form 2:	JKLB	MNLB	OPQB	RSQB	TUVQB	PBWB	XYB	HIB
Form 3:	JKC	MNC	OPD	RSD	TUVD	PBS	XZ	HG

A gifted young English architect named Michael Ventris (1922–56), who had studied classical and several modern European languages at an early age, heard Sir Arthur Evans discuss an exhibit of Minoan antiquities in 1936. The boy then and there conceived the goal of deciphering the Knossos tablets. In 1940 he published an article proposing

Etruscan affinities, nor did he completely shake off this notion until 1952, when he scored his breakthrough and deciphered Linear B. It was only after sixteen years of thought and frustrating labor that Ventris seriously considered the possibility that the language might be Greek after all.

Ventris reasoned that since Forms 1 and 2 of the above eight words were adjectives, they might well tell the places from which the people came, in which case Form 3 would be the place name itself without any adjectival suffix.

Now, derived feminine names ending in -*i(y)a* occur in Greek as well as in other languages around the Mediterranean. Therefore, A might be read *ya*, and the preceding signs (L, Q, W, Y, and I) would end in -*i*. T happens to be of very high frequency, especially at the beginning of words; it should therefore be a vowel, probably *a*, which in many languages, including Greek, is the commonest vowel that begins words. It is also clear from the short spelling in Form 3 that the consonant of the case ending (-*s*) was not written.

Ventris asked himself, "What well-known towns in ancient Crete can be matched with JKC, MNC, OPD, RSD, and TUVD?" If T = *a* and TUVD has three syllables after the *a*-, the town of Amniso(s) comes to mind, so that TUVD is presumably to be transliterated *A-mi-ni-so*, and TUVQA = *A-mi-ni-si-ya*. The masculine of the latter, TUVQB, can then only be *A-mi-ni-si-yo*. 𐀀 𐀖 𐀛 𐀰 , *a-mi-ni-so* (Amnisos), was the initial reading that opened Ventris's decipherment of Linear B.

The fact that *A-mi-ni-so* ends in -*o* suggests that other place names may end similarly. Therefore, while L, Q, W, Y, and I end in -*i*, the following have the same respective consonants but end in -*o;* C, D, S, Z, and G. Now S appears not only as the final syllable in the name PBS but as the second syllable in RSD; the latter is therefore a town name of three syllables ending in -*oso*. *Ko-no-so* (Knossos) is the obvious reading because the tablets where this name is found all come from Knossos (and none from the mainland tablets of Pylos and Mycenae). This gives us R = *ko* and S = *no*. The next question is, "What other Cretan town, preferably not too far from Knossos, has three consonants and ends in -*so* (for No. III, OPD, ends in D = *so*)?" Ventris's choice of Tuliso(s) (Tylissos) proved to be correct and so yielded O = *tu,* P = *li/ri.*

The character of the Cypriot syllabary was always in the background of the decipherment of Linear B. Actually, seven signs have the same form and sound in the two systems; one of them is the *pa* sign (a vertical line crossed by two horizontals), which we have represented as M in MNC (No. II above). The Cretan town beginning with *Pa-* is Phaistos; this would yield *to* as the value for C (and hence *ti* as the value for L). N was eventually established as the vowel sign *i;* we have *Pa-i-to* for "Phaistos" (for *s* never appears at the close of the syllable). The first name JKC has to be another Cretan town with a name of three consonants ending in in -*to;* Lukto(s) (Lyktos), surmised by Ventris, was right, yielding J = *lu/ru* and K = *ki* (where the silent vowel fits in perfectly for Forms 1 and 2; *Lu-ki-ti-ya* and *Lu-ki-ti-yo*).

Ventris shrewdly surmised that certain designations common to Pylos and Knossos might refer to guilds, whereas parallel designations limited to either Pylos or Knossos were toponyms (unaugmented or adjectivalized). The names of guilds and towns were to be expected on the analogy of administrative texts from Ugarit.

The phonetic values established by Ventris enabled him to detect Greek words, including some that had been interpreted correctly (although not pronounced nor identified linguistically) by other scholars. For example, Kober had shown that what we now read as *to-so* accompanies totals of masculine entries (of men or male animals), whereas what we now read as *to-sa* accompanies totals of feminine entries. Ventris could now read them as Greek *tosoi* (masculine plural) and *tosai* (feminine plural) "so many." Moreover, Kober had straightened out the genders of the words we now read as *ko-wo* "boy," and *ko-wa* "girl" (first identified by Cowley, albeit with the genders confused). In accordance with the orthographic rules formulated by Ventris, *ko-wo* and *ko-wa* stood for dialectal Greek *korwo-s* "boy" and *korwa* "girl."[6]

After the decipherment of Linear B as Greek had been accomplished, and the phonetic values ascertained by Ventris were known in the circle of professional Mycenologists, Carl Blegen noted a Linear B tablet unearthed by his expedition at Pylos. It is an inventory of different sorts of pots, with each category described syllabically as well as depicted graphically by a determinative. The latter shows whether the pot is a vase or a tripod and whether it has three, four, or no handles. Applying Ventris's values to the syllabic signs, Blegen found that the verbal descriptions fit the accompanying pictographs in Greek. An examination of the tablet shows that a tripod pictograph followed by the numeral 1 is labelled *ti-ri-po* = Greek *tripou(s)* "tripod," whereas the same pictograph followed by the numeral 2 is spelled *ti-ri-po-de* = *tripode*—the exact dual form in classi-

6. For the large growing literature pertaining to Linear A and B, see *Nestor*, issued monthly at the University of Wisconsin in Madison, Wisconsin.

cal Greek. Vessels with no handles are described on the Pylos tablet as *a-no-we* "without handle," those with three handles as *ti-ri-yo-we* "three-handled," and those with four handles as *qe-to-ro-we* "four-handled." The prefixed *a(n)-* "without" and *tri-* "three" are perfect Greek; "four" is dialectal and looks more like Latin *quattuor* than standard Greek *tetra-*, but no one should expect Mycenaean Greek to be exactly like any particular previously known dialect.

Ventris's decipherment of Linear B as Greek was not only well done but in general well received. The confirmation supplied by the "virtual bilingual" from Pylos came at just the right time to convince many who might otherwise have hesitated. To be sure, a few doubting Thomases still refuse to accept the testimony of the Pylos tablet, and one scholar went so far as to accuse Ventris of clandestine knowledge of the Pylos tablet. The implication was that Ventris had based his decipherment on that tablet, and therefore his phonetic values had been contrived to describe the pots. Anyone who knows the integrity of Ventris and Blegen cannot imagine them engaging in anything even remotely smacking of skulduggery. There are always those who believe exactly what they want to believe, facts notwithstanding. It is a mistake to take obscurantists too seriously, no matter how learned they happen to be.

The quick general acceptance of Ventris's decipherment was due also to the desire of those raised in the classical tradition to enhance the glory of Greece. Not that there was ever any reason to doubt that Achilles, Agamemnon, or Nestor spoke Greek. But archaeologists had come up with all kinds of theories, and the prestige of Sir Arthur Evans had lent much weight to the notion that Linear A and B were not Greek. Therefore, though Ventris's decipherment was a surprise, it was a welcome and pleasant surprise to Hellenophiles. And what civilized person is not Hellenophile?

The sudden death of Michael Ventris in a car accident on 6 September 1956 snuffed out the life of a talented and fortunate young man. He died after succeeding in his life-work, having received recognition and due honors at home and abroad. The mopping-up operation is being completed by others.

We now come to Linear A. Of all the deciphered inscriptions, it is Minoan Linear A that will continue to shed the most light on our own classical origins. Greek civilization is, from preclassical times, closely intertwined with West Semitic elements, ranging from vocabulary to social institutions. Minoan Linear A indicates that much of the Semitic component in ancient Greece was due not only to borrowing from the outside but also to an influential substratum on the Greek soil, before Greece was Greek. The Greeks themselves attributed their alphabet to the Phoenicians through Semitic princes such as Cadmus, who became king of Boeotian Thebes. His name, which is derived from Semitic *Cadm-* "East" is the counterpart of the name of his sister Europa, for *Europ-* (like Hebrew *ʿereb*) designates "West." By telling us that the mother of Minos was the Semitic princess Europa, the Greeks have prepared us for recognizing the Semitic character of the mother tongue of the Minoans.

Most of the names (and some of the common nouns) ending in *-eus* in ancient Greek lore are not of Greek origin. For example, Pers-eus is derived from the Semitic root *p-r-s* "to cut": appropriate for the hero who is famed for cutting off the head of the Gorgon, Medusa.

Scientific method does not permit us to accept Greek tradition uncritically. We must ultimately base the identification of the Minoan language on the Linear A inscriptions themselves. The corpus of Minoan inscriptions is not among the greatest troves of excavated texts, quantitatively or literarily. So far there are no Minoan epics or historical documents. Instead the Minoan Linear A inscriptions comprise a few hundred small administrative tablets containing little more than proper names, common nouns for commodities, and numerals. Almost the only sentence structure is supplied by a score of short dedicatory inscriptions on votive offerings. It is not even certain that all the so-called Linear A texts are in the same language. However, since the cultic dedications at a wide variety of Cretan sites employ the same formulae, we can at least define Minoan as the one language, in Linear A writing, used at all the Minoan shrines of Crete where such texts have been found so far.

Though the Minoan inscriptions are jejune and formulaic, they are of paramount importance because they record the language of Europe's first great and literate civilization. The Mycenaeans patterned their culture after the Minoan model and expressed their Greek language in a variation of the Minoan script. The textually documented origins of Western culture on European soil accordingly go back to Minoan Linear A in the Middle Bronze Age.

The Minoan problem has two intertwined factors: script and language. The Linear A and Linear B syllabaries are essentially the same, as indicated by the same proper names that appear in both sets of inscriptions.[7] Basically, the pronunciation of the phonetic values of the Linear A signs

---

7. For such fundamentals the reader is referred to my *Evidence for the Minoan Language* (Ventnor, N.J.: Ventnor Publishers, 1966) and "The Decipherment of Minoan and Eteocretan," *Journal of the Royal Asiatic Society* (1975): 148–58.

were provided by the decipherment of Linear B by Michael Ventris.[8] It was the Minoan language that still required analysis, linguistic identification, and translation.

The best key to the Minoan language is the corpus of Eteocretan inscriptions, which, though late (the sixth to fourth centuries B.C.), are written alphabetically and can therefore be pronounced without esoteric knowledge. It has been correctly assumed that the Eteocretans were the remnant of the Minoans and that the Eteocretan inscriptions are written in a late stage of the Minoan language.[9] It was clear that although Eteocretan was written in the same alphabet as Greek, it was a totally different language (even as Linear A and B, though essentially the same script, recorded entirely different languages). The corpus of inscribed Eteocretan stones from Praisos, Dreros, and Psychro in eastern Crete is the logical starting place for the decipherment of Minoan. For Eteocretan has always been at least pronounceable, whereas Linear A was not until Ventris's breakthrough in 1952; and, even since then, several Linear A syllabic signs continue to require phonetic clarification.[10]

The further we go back in time during the Early Iron and Late and Middle Bronze Ages, the more evidence we find for the presence of Northwest Semites in the Aegean.[11] The facts of the case are sometimes startling. In a standard corpus of the major Phoenician texts, eight come

8. The achievement of Ventris was a decipherment in the strictest sense of the word: the solution of a hitherto unknown script followed by the translation of the texts. Linear A was no longer a totally unknown script once B was deciphered.

9. N. G. L. Hammond, *A History of Greece to 322 B. C.*, 2d ed. (Oxford: Clarendon Press, 1967), pp. 69, 82.

10. Such signs include syllables with Semitic consonants not used in Mycenean Greek.

11. Genesis 9:27 could refer to the Greek takeover from the Semites there.

from Athens-Piraeus, as opposed to four from Sidon and only one from Tyre![12]

We have just used the term "Phoenician" in its precise modern and academically approved connotation. The ancient Greeks, however, employed it in a broader sense; for them, "Phoenicians" referred to all varieties of Northwest Semitic merchant mariners who traded throughout and beyond the Mediterranean.

The testimony of the prologue to *Dictys Cretensis* is curious.[13] We know the text almost entirely from the Latin translation by Lucius Septimius in the fourth century A.D. It is a narrative proclaiming to be the composition of a Cretan hero, Dictys, who accompanied Idomeneus and Meriones to Troy. It is, of course, a pseudepigraphon, but it happens to be of interest for the Minoan problem.

The Latin translation of *Dictys Cretensis* is prefaced by a letter (*epistula*) as well as the prologue. The letter was composed by Lucius Septimius and addressed to Quintus Aradius Rufinus. It states that Dictys wrote "in Punic letters," and that the tomb of Dictys at Knossos had caved in from age with the result that a container sealed with tin became exposed. Shepherds chanced on the container and hoped to find treasure in it but found only sheets of inscribed lime bark, which they brought to the lord of the place, who was called Praxis. Since the language was Greek, he transcribed the letters into Attic and presented the sheets to the Emperor Nero, who rewarded him handsomely. Thus, according to the *epistula*, Lucius Septimius considered the original a Greek work written in Punic

12. H. Donner and W. Röllig, *Kanaanäische und aramäische Inschriften* (Wiesbaden: Harrassowitz, 1962), pp. V, 2, 3, 13.

13. For text, translation, and commentary, see Howard J. Marblestone, "Dictys Cretensis: A Study of the Ephemeris Belli Troiani as a Cretan Pseudepigraphon" (Ph.D. diss., Brandeis University, 1970).

script. If we were to defend this opinion, we could point to Greek inscriptions of the Archaic Period, in which the letter-forms still closely resemble the Phoenician letters from which the Greek alphabet was derived.

The prologue, unlike the letter, is not the work of Lucius Septimius, but rather the prologue to the Greek text that he merely rendered into Latin. For this reason its testimony is older and closer to the facts than the *epistula*. The prologue relates that Dictys was a Cretan from Knossos, an expert in the Phoenician language, both spoken and written. He is represented as a comrade of Idomeneus and Meriones, who commissioned him to write the annals of the Trojan War, which he set down on lime bark. His annals, comprising nine volumes, were placed in a tin chest and buried with him at his behest.

In the thirteenth year of Nero's reign (A.D. 66)—so the prologue continues—earthquakes at Knossos played havoc with many tombs, including that of Dictys, with the result that the tin chest was exposed to view. Shepherds saw and took it but, upon opening it, found only lime bark in a script unknown to them. So they brought the document to their master Eupraxides, who, being also unfamiliar with the script, offered it to the Roman consular official of the island, Rutilius Rufus. He dispatched Eupraxides to Nero with the text. Nero, observing that the letters were Punic, called in experts who interpreted everything. When Nero thus learned that the document was composed by an ancient who had been at Troy, he ordered it to be translated into Greek for his Greek library.

We need not discuss all the discrepancies between the letter and the prologue. But we must note that, according to the prologue, not only the script but also the language of the original was "Punic," a term used interchangeably with "Phoenician." This calls to mind the Eteocretan inscriptions which, as we shall see, are in Northwest Semitic and recorded in "Phoenician/Punic" letter-forms in the Archaic Period.

Nineteenth-century scholars suspected the annals of Dictys Cretensis to be a fraud and having been composed by Lucius Septimius in Latin. But the discovery in Egypt of papyri, antedating the lifetime of Lucius Septimius, with parts of the Greek text of Dictys, makes it clear that no fraud was perpetrated by Lucius Septimius. The question accordingly is not, Was the Latin translated from a Greek text? but rather, Was the Greek translated from a Semitic original?

In Hellenistic times there was a literary movement among the Northwest Semites to fill in the gaps of "canonical"[14] scripture through pseudepigrapha. The documentation is richest among the Jews. *The Book of Enoch* and *The Testaments of the Twelve Patriarchs* are cases in point. Such pseudepigrapha are now attested in their Hebrew originals at Qumran in collections copied and assembled in Roman times before and a few years after Nero's reign. But they are compositions of an earlier Hellenistic age. The same movement that produced apocrypha and pseudepigrapha in Jewish circles, extended among the Northwest Semites across "denominational"[15] lines to the Eteocretans, whose "canonical scripture" was not the Bible, but Homeric epic. Then, as indeed today, the Cretans remained "ethnocentric" vis-à-vis the rest of the Greek world. It was "in character" for the Eteocretans to glorify the Cretan role in the Trojan War.

---

14. "Canonical" is a descriptive and useful, albeit anachronistic term. The Old Testament canon was not officially fixed until about A.D. 100. But such official steps only formalized long-held attitudes.

15. Another descriptive and useful anachronism.

The prologue to the annals of Dictys indicates that Semitic Eteocretan was not only written in Crete (which we know to be a fact from the Eteocretan inscriptions themselves), but that at least into the first century A.D. the nature of Eteocretan was familiar to the intelligentsia of Rome, including the Emperor Nero.

In our time, both Eteocretan and Minoan required linguistic identification. While Minoan is recorded in the problematic Linear A syllabary, Eteocretan is in the familiar alphabet. It makes sense to start with the Eteocretan inscriptions, where at least the script is fully known, and work backwards chronologically into the Minoan texts couched in the more difficult Linear A.

The Cretan town of Praisos[16] had a population divided into two linguistic groups: Greek and Eteocretan. Each group wrote texts in its own language. Since the Greek and the Eteocretan texts came from the same time and place, they overlap in content. For example, a Greek inscription from Praisos contains this adjuratory formula: $\tau[o\grave{v}\varsigma \; \overset{?}{\alpha}\lambda\lambda o]v\varsigma \; \pi o\lambda\acute{\iota}\tau\alpha\varsigma \; \overset{?}{\epsilon}\xi o\rho\kappa\iota\tilde{\omega} \; \tau o\grave{v}[\varsigma \; \overset{?}{\epsilon}v]\delta\acute{\alpha}\mu ov[\varsigma \; \mu\grave{\epsilon}v \; . \; . \;]$ $\tau o\grave{v}\varsigma \; \delta'\overset{?}{\alpha}\pi o\delta\acute{\alpha}\mu ov\varsigma$ ("I shall adjure the various citizens, both the natives and the foreigners"). This formula employs a merism to express "everybody"; to wit, the pair of antonyms "in-people" (natives) and "out-people" (foreigners). Variants of idioms to express "everybody" are common in the inscriptions of the ancient East Mediterranean.[17] Two of them occur in Eteocretan texts from Praisos. What we can learn from them is best brought out by aligning them one above the other:

16. At Dreros, a similarly mixed Cretan community, were found two Greco-Eteocretan bilingual texts. See also my "Greek and Eteocretan Unilinguals from Praisos and Dreros," *Berytus* 19 (1970): 95–98.
17. Gordon, "Minoan and Eteocretan," pp. 150–51.

1. μαρ κρκ-ο   κλ ες υ ες[   ]
2. νας   ιρ-ο υ κλ ες

The first variant is literally "lord of his fortress, every man, and man [of   ]." The second means "people of his city and every (other) man." The vocabulary, possessive pronominal suffix, and syntax are, in their totality, Northwest Semitic: *Mâr* "lord" (Aramaic); *kark-*"walled town" (Aramaic; also the first element in Καρχηδών, the Greek name for Carthage); *-ô* "his" (as in Hebrew); *kull* "all, every" (attested earlier in Minoan); *'eš* "man" (as in Eshbaal "Man-of-Baal"; the more familiar form is Hebrew *'îš* "man"); *û* "and" (already attested in Minoan); *nâš* "people" (occurs in Arabic *nâš;* and in the Syriac *qrê, bar-nâš* "son of mankind," "a human being"); and *'îr* "city" (common in Hebrew; occurs also in Ugaritic). *Mâr k(a)rk* and *nâš îr* are a synonymous pair of compound idioms, all four nouns of which exist together only in Northwest Semitic.

One of the Eteocretan inscriptions can be translated with reasonable certainty in all but one of its details.[18] It is the Psychro Stone of about 300 B.C. found at the Dictyan Cave where Minoan objects have been recovered showing that the living tradition among the natives that the cave is Zeus's birthplace goes back to Minoan times. The Psychro text is important on several counts. It ends with three late forms of Linear A signs, proving that at Psychro there was continuity from Minoan to Eteocretan. Furthermore, the

18. The interpretation is subject to the disputed identity of the fourth letter in the first line. I take it (with all due reservation) to be theta, as it was first read in the *editio princeps* by Spyridon Marinatos, "Grammátōn didaskália," *Minoica* (Festschrift for Johannes Sundwall) (1958): 226–31 (and pl. I). Some scholars would now read it as omicron. The only distinction between theta and omicron, in this inscription, is the dot inside the theta. A member of the Heraklion Museum staff kindly has collated the text for me and reports that the dot is no longer clearly visible so that it is now impossible to tell whether the letter is omicron or theta.

text is a lapidary votive inscription like so many of the Linear A dedications on stone cult objects. The Psychro Stone carries on the conservative tradition of Minoan *ex voto* formulae. It runs as follows:

1. ΕΠΙΘΙ
2. ΖΗΘΑΝΘΗ
3. ΕΝΕΤΗ ΠΑΡ ΣΙΦΑΙ
4. Ψ ⟁ ⟰

An idiomatic English translation is: "I, Enetê son of Siphai, have presented this engraved stone." In line 4, the first and third syllabic signs are fairly certain; they are *i* and *ti* respectively. The middle sign possibly could be *pi*, in which case *i-pi-ti* would repeat the word in line 1 (ἐπιθι). But if the sign is read *ne*, the resultant reading *i-ne-ti* (the name of the donor, Enetê) seems more likely. In line 1 the lapidary nature of the text favors translating πιθι as "engraved stone" (the Phoenician פתח "engraved stone"), anticipated by Minoan *pi-te* on a votive stone cult object.[19] The ε- would then be the definite article (*ha-* in Hebrew). Since the definite article came in with the advent of the Iron Age, it is lacking in Minoan and Ugaritic. Z in Line 2 is either the postpositive demonstrative pronoun "this" (written as -z in Phoenician) or the prepositive relative pronoun "which" (written as z- in Phoenician). While its position in line 2 might suggest the latter, I prefer the former, not so much because there is no room for it on the preceding line in any case, but in Linear A it is definitely suffixed in *pi-te-za* "this engraved stone." ΗΘΑΝΘΗ is יתנתי , *yatan-tî* 'I have given." For the verb יתן "to give" (as a votive offering) and the suffix -*tî* to indicate the

19. Gordon, *Evidence*, pp. 13–14.

pronominal subject "I" with the perfect, we may turn not only to Phoenician but also to Minoan dedicatory formulae.[20] The interpretation of line 3 we owe to Robert R. Stieglitz,[21] who recognized that παρ is the Aramaic *bar* "son" and that Σιφαι is a personal name (סַפַּי) occurring in 1 Chronicles 20:4.

The Minoan texts are more difficult to interpret than the Eteocretan, largely because as we have already observed, the Linear A script is unfamiliar to Semitists. Like the Akkadian syllabary, Linear A indicates the vowels, though neither system makes all the consonantal distinctions that we are used to from the alphabet. HT 31 is a good starting point for deciphering Minoan Linear A because on HT 31 various pictographs of bowls and other vessels appear that are accompanied by superscript words spelled out syllabically. Indeed it occurred to early investigators of Linear B that the syllabic superscriptions on HT 31 are the Minoan words for the depicted vessels. Since the HT 31 vessel names include *su-pu*, *su-pà-la*[22] (compare סף and ספל in Hebrew and other Semitic languages) and *ka-ro-pà* (compare *karpu*, a vessel name in Akkadian), this text is a key to the Semitic character of Minoan. HT 31 can be translated to the extent that it is preserved. In the transliteration are code numbers for the vessel pictograms, while the superscript names are given in the translation.

1. *mi-ti-sa . pu-ko* . Lc45
2. [*x*]+4 Lc63 *10* Lc64 *10*

20. Note especially *ya-ta-no-* or *a-ta-no-* "he has given." See Gordon, *Evidence*, pp. 28, 37.
21. Robert R. Stieglitz, "The Eteocretan Inscription from Psychro," *Kadmos* 15 (1976): 84–86.
22. Linear A does not distinguish *l-* from *r-* syllables. Usually scholars transliterate with *r-*, to the exclusion of *l-*, regardless of etymology. To avoid linguistic confusion, *la* is used rather than *ra* here, because this word for "vessel" appears as *spl* in Ugaritic (and similarly in other Semitic languages).

3. [   ] Lc63 *10 sa-ya-ma-na*
4. [   ] *ki-de-ma-wi-na*
5. ? ? L'9 [x+] *300* Lc66 *300*
6. Lc67 *3000*

1. Go out from the depot! [x] tri-
2. pods, 10 *qa-pà* vessels, 10 *su-pu* vessels,
3. [   ], 10 silver pitchers,
4. [x] golden [vases],
5. [x+]300 [?]-vessels, 300 *su-pà-la* vessels,
6. 3000 *pa-ta-qe* cups.

Roberta Richard[23] was the first to point out that HT 31 is an order to issue vessels from a repository. The *crux interpretum* that she solved was *pu-ko* (the plural Aramaic פקו "go out"!), though she felt constrained to give it a causative meaning ("bring out"!). However, Minoan usage, in agreement with Ugaritic, permits one to speak of merchandise as "going out" rather than being "brought out" by somebody.[24] Once the verb was recognized as "to go out," the *mi-* (in the preceding word that opens the tablet) was seen to be the West Semitic preposition "from." While Ms. Richard has made a case for *ti-sa* "depot, treasury," other possibilities should be kept in mind for the time being. It is unnecessary to belabor the Semitic identifications of the vessel names because the data have long ago been set forth in detail.[25] It should be noted, however, that a Minoan magic bowl begins with *a-ga-nu*[26] (equals *'aggânu* "bowl" in Aramaic, Hebrew, Akkadian, and other Semitic dialects).[27]

23. Roberta J. Richard, "HT 31—An Interpretation," *Kadmos* 13 (1974): 6–8.
24. Cyrus H. Gordon, "Further Notes on the Hagia Triada Tablet No. 31," *Kadmos* 15 (1976): 28–30.
25. For example, see Gordon, *Evidence*, p. 26.
26. Linear A and B do not distinguish *g* from *k*. Our *ga* is usually rendered *ka* in the transliteration. Cognate usage consistently points to *g* in this word.
27. See the list of Minoan vessel names in Armas Salonen, *Die Hausgeräte der*

Regardless of origin, כֶּסֶף (compare sa-ya-ma-na in HT
31:3) means "silver" in some Aramaic texts, while kidem in
the next line may well be the word for "gold" (ktm is "gold"
in Hebrew and Egyptian, and now also in Eblaite: ku₈-tim
"gold"). Ki-de-ma-wi-na (HT 31:4) has been analyzed as
kidem "gold" plus the adjective suffix -âwi plus the West
Semitic masculine plural suffix -îna. Some Semitic vessel
names are masculine, while others are feminine. If say(a)m-
"silver" is followed by the suffix -âna, we are confronted
with a distinctively Aramaic phenomenon: absolute masculine plural -îna versus absolute feminine plural -âna.[28]

Minoan words, fixed contextually, can be shown in specific cases to be Semitic. On a wine pithos is inscribed ya-ne
(yan is "wine" as in Ugaritic).[29] (Note the difference between yan and the more familiar yayn/yên.) The pithos
comes from Knossos where other wine pithoi are inscribed
with the WINE ideogram.

Twice the sequence ku-ni-su is followed by the WHEAT
determinative (therefore compare kun(n)išu "emmer wheat"
in Akkadian). The cognate occurs in Aramaic kunnəta (masculine) from *kunniṯ.[30]

(Y)a-sa-sa-la-mx occurs repeatedly but only on votive offerings. Derived from the root šlm that is the base for nouns
and verbs having to do with offerings, it may well mean "a
votive offering." Moreover it is used in the Š-conjugation
in Ugaritic. Sibilant causatives are found throughout
Egypto-Semitic.[31]

Totals are labeled ku-lo "all" not only in the HT corpus

alten Mesopotamien II: Gefässe (Helsinki: Finnish Academy of Sciences, 1966), p. 432.
  28. Cyrus H. Gordon, "Ki-de-ma-wi-na (HT 31:4)," Kadmos 8 1969: 131–33, and
Richard, "HT 31," pp. 66–67.
  29. Gordon, "Minoan and Eteocretan," pp. 157–58.
  30. Gordon, Evidence, p. 26, and Gordon, "Minoan and Eteocretan," p. 155.
  31. Gordon, Evidence, pp. 28, 37.

but also in the Linear tablets from Kato Zakro.[32] As pointed out above, this Common Semitic word (*kull-*) occurs also in Eteocretan.

On a libation table from Palaikastro *le ya-sa-*[   ] is probably to be restored *le ya-sa-[sa-la-mx]* "for a votive offering" with *le* equal to *la* West Semitic "to, for" (and for example, the Arabic *li-*). This preposition appears in Eteocretan ΛΜΟ corresponding to the dative ΜΑΤΡΙ "for mother" in a Greco-Eteocretan bilingual from Dreros.

One of the features of Minoan is the different nominal patterns of case endings. For example in HT 31, *su-pu* seems to be the nominative of a normal triptotic in -*u*, while *su-pà-la* looks like what Arabic grammarians call an indeclinable in -*a*. Eblaite is also characterized by such a variety of nominal endings that none of the publications so far makes any sense of it. Eblaite and Minoan suggest that in the Early and Middle Bronze Ages, there were Semitic dialects with varying categories of nominal inflections. Regularity may have been favored by force of analogy, so that by the time we find Ugaritic in the Late Bronze Age, the triptotic pattern had become the norm.

In summary, the Eteocretan texts are Northwest Semitic with strong Aramaic affinities. There is every reason to accept the long-held view that Minoan is the parent language of Eteocretan. The widely distributed votive texts in Linear A are in the same Semitic language that we may safely regard as the official language of Minoan civilization. Yet, until all of the Linear A tablets from all the sites where they have been found are interpreted, we must not jump to the conclusion that everything written in Linear A repre-

---

32. N. Platon and W. C. Brice, *Inscribed Tablets and Pithos in Linear A System from Zakro* (Athens: Library of the Archaeological Society, 1975), p. 73, text 12b:2.

sents the same language. (The same must be said for Linear B inscriptions; those that are not yet intelligible need not be in Mycenaean Greek.) The population of ancient Crete was mixed. Homer (*Odyssey* 19:175–7) records that it included Achaeans, Eteocretans, Kydonians, Dorians, and Pelasgians. To judge from the Linear A personal names, earlier, in Minoan times, there was also a considerable mixture: in addition to Semitic names, there were also Egyptian, Hurrian, and others.[33] So far, no Greek names have been detected, but there is no telling what future discoveries may bring.

The implications of the linguistic identity of Minoan are far-reaching. In the Iron Age intimate connections between Greece and the Near East were not always due to direct contacts between the two areas. The Near East had come to Greece and entrenched itself there both before and during the Bronze Age, before Greece was Greek. To a great extent, Greece did not have to go to the Near East; the Near East had already come to it.[34]

The difficulties in reading Minoan are due largely to the Aegean script. In interpreting and reconstructing Hittite and Eblaite, we are aided by the fact that their Mesopotamian cuneiform writing is a "known" quantity. But with Linear A the Aegean script is more problematic; and we may well be confronted with "Aegeograms" to be pronounced as Minoan. The "known" Sumerograms and Akkadograms in Hittite and Eblaite texts are aids in contrast with the obstacles posed by the "Aegeograms" in a still unknown language.

33. Gordon, *Evidence*, pp. 31–32.
34. Cyrus H. Gordon, *The Common Background of Greek and Hebrew Civilizations* (New York: Norton, 1965).

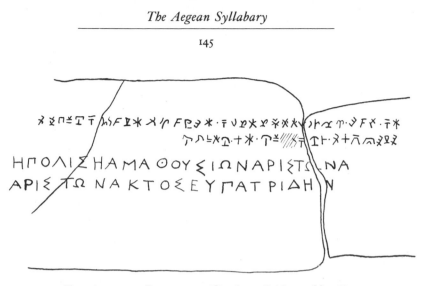

THE AMATHUS BILINGUAL. (Gordon, *Evidence*, §§5–6.)

THE FIRST DREROS BILINGUAL. The first two lines are Eteocretan and run retrograde. The last three lines are Greek and are boustrophedon. Note the corresponding IPMAF (Aramaic רמן "they established, decreed") corresponding to EFAΔE; and ΛMO (cf. Hebrew לאמנו "for his mother") corresponding to . . . MATPI . . . . (Gordon, *Evidence*, §§20–21.)

THE SECOND DREROS BILINGUAL. The first line is Eteocretan and ends
with IHIA (cf. Hebrew יהיה "it will be") corresponding to the final
Greek word ΓΕΝΟΙΤΟ "let there be." (Gordon, *Evidence*, §§28–29.)

THE EARLY (FIRST) PRAISOS TEXT. In lines 3–4 of this boustrophedon
text note ΜΑΡ ΚΡΚΟ ΚΛ ΕΣ Υ ΕΣ "lord of his city, every man and
man...." (Gordon, *Evidence*, §32.)

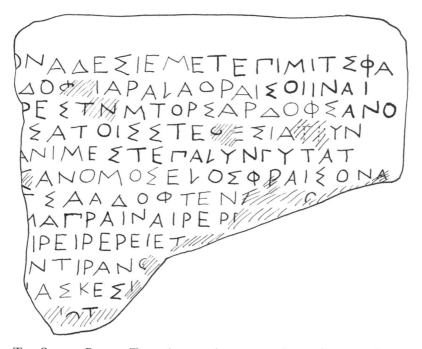

THE SECOND PRAISOS TEXT. Among the noteworthy readings are three numerals (each followed by the same word ΔΟΦ): ΣΦΑ[A] = שבעה "7" (lines 1–2), (TOP)ΣΑΡ = סר (תרי) (line 3) "10" (or "12"), and ΤΣΑΑ = תשעה "9" (line 7). (Gordon, *Evidence*, §34.)

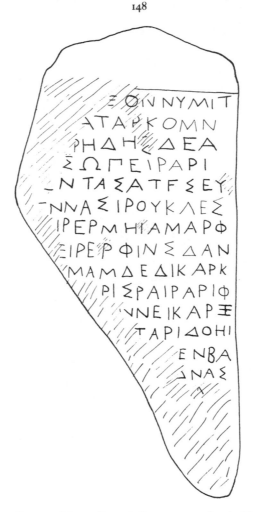

THE THIRD PRAISOS TEXT. Especially noteworthy is ΝΑΣ ΙΡΟ Υ ΚΛ ΕΣ "the people of his city and every (other) man" in line 6. (Gordon, *Evidence*, §39.)

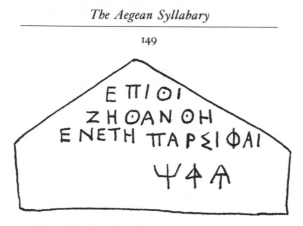

THE PSYCHRO TEXT. Updated and interpreted in the present chapter. (A collation of the text reveals that it is no longer possible to tell whether it is a theta or an omicron that is to read in line 1.) (Gordon, *Evidence,* §45.)

HT 31. Updated and interpreted in the present chapter. (Gordon, *Evidence,* §115.)

HT 86:a:1–2, b:1–2. *ku-ni-su* "emmer wheat" followed by WHEAT determinative. (Gordon, *Evidence*, §116.)

HT 88. Note that the six entries in lines 3–5 are each followed by a vertical line (the numeral "1") and are summed up at the end by *ku-lo* "all, total" followed by six vertical lines "6." (Gordon, *Evidence*, §117.)

HT 122:a:end

HT 122:b:end

From HT 122. A "total" (*ku-lo*) of "31" plus another of "65" yields a "grand total" (*po-to-ku-lo*) of "96." (Gordon, *Evidence*, §118.)

On Libation Bowl From Apodoulou (1,14). Note the conjunction *u* and connecting two verbs beginning with *ya-: ya-ta-no-x u ya-*[   ] "he donated it and [   ]." (Gordon, *Evidence*, §121.)

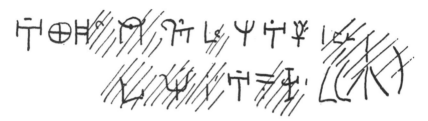

On Magic Cup From Knossos (II,2). The opening word *a-ga-nu* means "cup" in a number of Semitic languages including Aramaic. In the cuneiform Aramaic incantation from Uruk, this word is used in a magical context. (Gordon, *Evidence*, §§119, 156.)

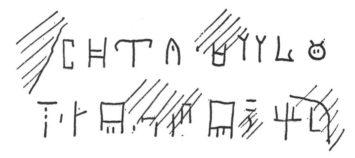

On Libation Table From Knossos (I,8). Note *ta-mu-a,ti ya-sa-sa-la-ma-na* "I set up this votive offering." (Gordon, *Evidence*, §122.)

On Wine Pithos From Knossos (II,3). The solitary word *ya-ne* "wine." (Gordon, *Evidence*, §123.)

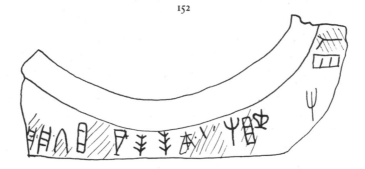

On Libation Table From Palaikastro (1,3). The last signs preserved (on the readers's right) are: *le ya-sa-*[   ] probably to be restored *le ya-sa-*[*sa-la-mx*] "for a votive offering." (Gordon, *Evidence*, §§125, 161.)

		A		E		I		O		U	
	a	干			i	屮			u	ρ
P	pa / pà	‡ / ⊟			pi	⋔			pu	⋩ (or) ⋩
T	ta / tá	匚 / ▽	te	⋇	ti	∧ (or) ∧	to	干	tu	⊕ (or) ○
D	da	┝	de	♀	di	⁝	do	ⴳ	du	⩍
K	ka	⊕	ke	米	ki	ⴲ (or) ⴲ	ko	◊	ku	⧛ (or) ⇗
"Q"	qa	ⴸ	qe	☺						
M	ma	ⴵ			mi	ⱱ			mu	ⴼ (or) ⴼ
N	na	Ī	ne / né	ⴺ / ⴾ	ni	ⴸ	no	ⱳ	nu	⊟
R	ra / rá	ⴵ (or) ⴵ / ⴵ	re	Ψ	ri	ⴿ	ro	╋	ru	ⴴ
S	sa	Y	se	ⴾ					su	Ρ
Z	za	ⴼ								
W	wa	ⴲ	we	ⴵ						
Y	ya	ⴲ								

Partial Grid of the Minoan Syllabary. (Gordon, *Evidence*, §§138–46 and Plate XI.)

8

THE EBLA ARCHIVES

In 1964 an Italian expedition under the direction of Professor Paulo Matthiae of the University of Rome began to excavate Tell Mardikh, a large mound about thirty-four miles south and slightly west of Aleppo.[1] A stone inscription found on the site revealed that in antiquity the city had been called "Ebla," which was well known in the Cuneiform World. The Akkadian con-

1. For a general, firsthand account of Ebla, see Paolo Matthiae, *Ebla: An Empire Rediscovered* (Garden City, N.Y.: Doubleday, 1981).

queror Naram-Sin boasted of capturing Ebla and burning its palace in the twenty-third century B.C.

A preview of the linguistic character of the vast archives soon to emerge from the palace ruins came in 1974 when an assemblage of forty-two clay tablets was found in a palace chamber. The script is Sumerian and most of the vocabulary consists of Sumerian words. The language of the texts, however, is generally the local Semitic dialect that we call Eblaite. The Sumerian words are as a rule Sumerograms, to be pronounced as their Eblaite equivalents.[2] Actually the Ebla tablets include bilingual lexical texts, which instruct us how to translate Sumerian words into Eblaite. One text, for example, informs us that Sumerian GUŠKIN "gold" equals the Eblaite *kutim*. Sumerian was deciphered long ago so that the meaning of GUŠKIN is familiar to cuneiformists. *Kutim* is the same word for "gold" that appears in Hebrew as *ketem* and in Egyptian hieroglyphs as *k-t-m*. It probably also occurs in Minoan as *kidem-*.

The Ebla archives include treaties and other historical tablets that tie in with Mari on the Middle Euphrates and with Akkad in the time of its kings from Sargon to his grandson Naram-Sin. Also at Ebla were found inscriptions bearing the titles of two Old Kingdom pharaohs, Chefren of the Fourth Dynasty, and Pepi I of the Sixth Dynasty. Thus the heyday of Ebla was contemporary with both the Pyramid Age of Egypt and the Akkad Dynasty of Mesopotamia. The Ebla excavations show that shortly after 2500 B.C., Syria was an outstanding center of urban and literate civilization between Sargonid Mesopotamia and Old King-

2. For the Eblaite texts, note especially the following books of Giovanni Pettinato: *Catalogo dei Testi Cuneiformi di Tell Mardikh—Ebla* (Naples: Istituto Universitario Orientale di Napoli, 1979); *Testi Amministrativi della Biblioteca L. 2769* (Naples: Istituto Universitario Orientali di Napoli, 1980); and *The Archives of Ebla* (Garden City, N.Y.: Doubleday, 1981).

dom Egypt. The long-known cultural ties between the Nile and the Twin Rivers now have a well-documented, connecting link in Syria-Palestine at Ebla.

The Ebla tablets already unearthed perhaps number around 15,000; in any event, there are over 10,000, though probably less than 20,000. Professor Giovanni Pettinato of the University of Rome has catalogued over 6,500 of them.[3] Many of the texts are well preserved and large; some have as many as thirty columns on each side with fifty lines to the column, totaling about 3,000 lines. Even though the columns are fairly narrow and the lines short, such texts are extraordinarily long.

Most of the texts are administrative lists, dealing with agriculture, industry, international trade, personnel, or cultic practices. Some, like the treaties, have historical interest. The literary tablets show that the impact of cuneiform tradition deep in the third millennium brought with it a literary heritage. Moreover, the lexical texts are of special value because the bilingual vocabularies are keys to the Eblaite language.

The Ebla archives exemplify the cultural symbiosis of Sumerians and Semites that is attested in Mesopotamia from the beginning of Sumerian writing at the dawn of the third millennium. While the Semitic languages and Sumerian belong to two entirely different divisions of speech, they were in contact with each other before the first texts appear around 3000 B.C. Sumerian, which was written before any known Semitic text, already has Semitic words imbedded in it; for example, *silim* "well-being, peace" (cognate with Hebrew *šālôm* and Arabic *salâm*). Sumerian DAM-GAR "merchant" (pronounced *tamkar* in Akkadian) is re-

3. The highest number in his *Catalogo* is Text 6641.

garded as an early loan from Semitic *m-k-r* "to sell or buy" (usually "to sell" in Hebrew). Early Sumerian loans in Semitic are familiar. Thus Sumerian É-GAL (É "house" plus GAL "big") "palace, temple" comes into Akkadian as *êkallu* and into Hebrew as *hêkāl*. Until recently Sumerian GU-ZA "chair, throne" was universally considered as borrowed into Semitic (Akkadian *kussû*, Hebrew *kissê'*, Arabic *kursî*, and so forth). Now, some scholars consider it a Semitic borrowing in Sumerian. Either way, it attests prehistoric contacts between Semites and Sumerians.

Sumerian MÁ-LAH₄ "sailor" (MÁ "boat" plus LAH₄ "to go" or "cause to go") is borrowed into Semitic (Akkadian MALLÂH, Hebrew and Arabic MALLÂH). Sumerian *na(n)-gar* "carpenter" has been borrowed into Semitic (for example, Hebrew *naggâr*, Arabic *najjâr*, and so forth) with other Sumerian loans and native Semitic roots in the *qattâl* formation (patterned after such loans) to indicate professions or occupations. Note, for instance, Hebrew *gazzâr* or Arabic *jazzâr* "butcher"; Arabic *baqqâl* "grocer"; and Hebrew *pehâr* (from **pahhâr*) "potter" or *nahâg* (from **nahhâg*) "driver, chauffeur." This formation is interesting in that it is Sumerian in origin and became a common nominal type in Semitic.

Whatever the contribution of the Semites to early Sumerian civilization, it cannot diminish the primacy of the Sumerians as the first known speech-group in the world to establish a literate culture; and, moreover, one that was to remain classical for a galaxy of important offshoots for three thousand years. The Sumerian legacy goes on through its loanwords in Hebrew. Sumerian loanwords in Arabic keep spreading with the growth of Islam among Turkic, Persian, Urdu, Indonesian, and other speech-groups.

Ebla shows that its region had been intellectually Sumerianized. The Early Bronze Age archives of Ebla in Sumerian script indicate that the local scribes were schooled in the intricacies of Sumerology. This points to a Sumerian lingua franca, antedating the Amarna Age by a millennium, by which time Babylonian had become the international language of the Near East. How are we to account for this role of Sumerian in the Early Bronze Age? (Syria is fairly distant from Sumer in southern Iraq.)

There are two ways of approaching the Sumerian problem, and we can learn from both of them. First is the conventional way: Sumerian developed into a written medium in Sumer (Southern Babylonia), flourished throughout the third millennium, and was thereafter fostered as the classical language of the Assyro-Babylonian world. During the third millennium, certain rulers of Sumerian city-states embarked on spectacular conquests extending to the shores of the east Mediterranean. The best known of those Sumerian conquerors is Lugalzaggesi of Umma who forged his ephemeral empire only to be vanquished by Sargon of Akkad around 2300 B.C. during the period when scribes at Ebla were writing the tablets found there. We hardly can attribute the Sumerianism at Ebla to Lugalzaggesi's conquests in Syria, which in any case would be too recent to account for the depth of Sumerian tradition at Ebla. To the contrary, it is likely that Sumerianism had been gaining momentum for some time under the initiative of Mesopotamian merchants famed for their development of foreign trade. Yet there is always the possibility that armies had to some extent paved the way for the traders. We must not deny some kernel of historicity to Mesopotamian traditions that earlier rulers of Sumerian city-states, notably Lugal-anne-mundu of Adab, had carved out an empire stretching to the Mediterranean around the twenty-sixth century B.C.—six generations before Lugalzaggesi.

There is another, quite different way of approaching the Sumerian problem. The Sumerians could not have originated in Sumer. Their language is unrelated to any speech in the region and their way of life required minerals, both metals and stones, that never existed in Sumer. A suggestive discovery was made early in the 1960s at Tartaria in Rumanian Transylvania. There archaeologists found a few inscribed clay tablets whose shapes and writing resemble the most archaic tablets of Sumer. Carbon 14 tests on organic materials associated with the tablets point to a date around 2700 B.C. The minerals of Transylvania, including gold, provide a possible inducement that would have attracted people like the Sumerians. While the Sumerians required gold (whether from Nubia, Arabia, Transylvania, or anywhere else), they also needed an assortment of other minerals including lapis lazuli, which was presumably imported from Badakhshan in eastern Afghanistan. That Sumerian civilization required raw materials from great distances in different directions confronts us with an alternate view of Sumerian origins: that there was a loose, far-flung network of operational outposts for securing various raw materials to be processed at a "national"[4] center. In prehistoric times the center shifted, eventually to be located (around 3500 B.C.) in the land we call Sumer.

The selection of Sumer was favored by a number of considerations. The land is well watered by the Tigris and the Euphrates. Those rivers with the canal systems

---

4. The adjective "national" is descriptive and useful even though it is anachronistic so long before the age of nationalisms.

along and between them provided shipping lanes as well as fish and agricultural products. Sumer is bordered on the south by the Persian Gulf which opens onto the Indian Ocean with all its maritime trade. The limited natural resources of the land itself were augmented by the proximity of the mineral wealth of Iran, Arabia, and the mountainous terrain to the north. The Twin Rivers were gateways to many desiderata. Thus the Euphrates provided water routes for a good part of the way to the forests of the Lebanon, Anti-Lebanon, and Amanus mountains. Aside from the agricultural wealth of Sumer, the land has an abundant, though unprepossessing, commodity: mud, since the rivers bring down from the north vast quantities of silt. The Sumerians used mud brick as their primary building material and clay tablets as their main writing material. Wherever Sumerian and Babylonian civilization spread, the clay tablet inscribed with a stylus went with it.

Ebla by about 2500 B.C. had become an outlier[5] of the Sumerian Order. Simplification of the complex Sumerian problem serves a useful purpose provided that we remember it is only a first step in the quest for understanding something bigger than we can now fully grasp. The standard way of viewing the outposts of Sumerianism (which explains much, if not all, of the story) starts with the Sumerians in Sumer with an economy that required foreign trade for securing raw materials that it then processed. In exchange, it exported agricultural and animal products as well as manufactured wares. To maintain such a system, mercantile colonies had to be set up in peripheral areas. In

---

5. This term for a satellite community is familiar to certain groups of archaeologists, especially those working in southwestern states such as New Mexico and Arizona.

the more remote colonies, Sumerianization tended to be more attentuated. Hand in hand with the spread of Sumerianism to the foreign outposts came the influence of the peripheral cultures back to Sumer.

The colonies required personnel to keep the business records. For the cuneiform scribes, Sumerian remained the ultimate classical language, even after they applied Sumerian script to record various "barbaric" languages. Among the latter, Semitic Akkadian was the foremost; Hittite comes next in importance; and Hurrian must be rated high on the list, for it was the language of the powerful Mitanni kingdom during the early part of the Amarna Age. Hurrian texts have been found at major sites such as Mari, Ugarit, and Amarna. The Nuzu population was essentially Hurrian, while also at Alalakh and Ugarit there were large Hurrian minorities. Clay tablets inscribed with cuneiform include records of lost languages such as the Semitic dialects of Ugarit and, now, Ebla.

Sumerian may be the first of the linguae francae on record, but it is not the only one. It was followed by Akkadian and subsequently by Aramaic, which served as international languages. Let us start with Aramaic; for, in dealing with ancient history, there can be advantages in working from the later "better known" back to the earlier "less known." Aramaic as a common language in later Old Testament times is fully documented.

During Sennacherib's invasion of Judah in 701 B.C., the general public in Jerusalem spoke only Hebrew, though their diplomats could also use Aramaic as the lingua franca in negotiating with foreign officials. When the spokesmen of King Hezekiah wanted the Assyrian representative to speak Aramaic to keep the public from understanding the alarming Assyrian ultimatum, the Assyrian insisted on using Hebrew precisely so that the public would know what was going on.[6]

Aramaic made steady gains internationally. The Achaemenian Empire of the Medes and the Persians (the sixth to fourth centuries B.C.) used it as the interprovincial medium of communication beyond the Iranian homeland. Thus in the fifth century B.C. the agents of the Achaemenian emperors in the distant province of Egypt employed Aramaic. Functioning as an outpost of the Achaemenian Empire, the Jewish colony at Elephantine in Upper Egypt used it for correspondence and other documents. The Achaemenian age also evoked the Aramaic portions of Ezra and Daniel.

Aramaic expanded as a lingua franca, becoming the medium of both much rabbinic literature and a considerable segment of Eastern Christianity.[7] Pagans also fostered Aramaic dialects; for example, pagan Syriac literature and the whole corpus of Mandaic writings.

The wide use of Aramaic was always familiar in learned Judeo-Christian circles. But it was not until 1887 that the Amarna Letters began to come to light in Egypt. Those letters, from the reigns of Amenophis III (c. 1417–1379) and Amenophis IV (Akhenaton, c. 1379–62), are in Babylonian, even though they were exchanged between the two pharaohs on the one hand and the rulers of a wide variety of Near East regions on the other. Those regions embraced Syria-Palestine, Mesopotamia, Anatolia, and Cyprus. Many familiar sites in Israel are included: Jerusalem, Megiddo, Taanach, Ascalon, Gaza, Acre, and so forth. Although Babylonian was not the native language of Egypt,

6. 2 Kings 18:26–28.
7. Most of the texts written in Christian Aramaic dialects are classified as "Syriac."

Syria-Palestine, Anatolia, or Cyprus, it had gained the status of a common language throughout those (and still other) widely diversified areas.

The Amarna Tablets are far from the only witnesses of the Babylonian lingua franca during the Late Bronze Age (1600–1200 B.C.). One of the best documented witnesses is Ugarit (c. 1400–1200) on the north Syrian coast. The cuneiform tablets of Ugarit fall into two main categories: (1) the alphabetic texts in the local Ugaritic language, and (2) the syllabic archives in Babylonian. Diplomatic correspondence and treaties are normally in the international medium, Babylonian.

The classical language of Babylonia was Sumerian, and as long as Babylonian survived (into the first century A.D.), its scribes looked upon Sumerian much as Western Europe looks back on Latin. In Ugarit the scribes copied and studied quadrilingual vocabularies in which words of the same meaning were entered, each in four parallel columns: Sumerian, Babylonian, Hurrian, and Ugaritic. Ugaritic was the main language, and Hurrian the next most important, spoken by the local and regional populations. Babylonian was the lingua franca; but Sumerian was still cherished as the classical tongue of the ecumene.

Genesis 11:1–9 records a tradition about developments "after the Deluge"[8] or in modern terms "at the dawn of history." It relates that in land of Shinar,[9] the construction of a great city and tower[10] was being accomplished by a vast work force united through a single language used through-

---

8. Genesis 10:32.
9. In spite of the phonetic complexities involved in the Hebrew transliteration of Sumerian words, the Hebrew *šinᶜār* "Babylonia" may represent *šumer* "Sumer."
10. Genesis 11:3 specifies that the building material was baked brick, the Sumero-Babylonian material used for building the city walls and ziggurats.

out the earth. In modern parlance this means "an international lingua franca." This, however, is not to say that there was only one language in existence up to that time, because the preceding chapter of Genesis (10:5, 20:31) says that the various groupings of mankind, living in different countries, had their own languages. Accordingly, the "one language" does not signify that only one speech was used at home by all members of mankind, but rather that in the entire ecumene, there was a common tongue that made international projects possible.

The legend has it that insufferable arrogance went with such mighty projects, whose builders were out to reach the very heavens. God put an end to this hubris by breaking up the ecumene through terminating the lingua franca. Lacking the means of communication, the international order split into its component parts.

What was that common language? It could not have been Aramaic, which as a lingua franca was too late for the wondrous Mesopotamian constructions just "after the Flood." Babylonian is a conceivable candidate. Yet a tradition about the state of affairs "after the Flood" should refer back to a remote antiquity. And the Ebla tablets strongly suggest that Sumerian was the lingua franca "after the Flood."

The reconstruction of Eblaite is a slow process requiring judgment as well as familiarity with both many tablets and a wide range of Semitic languages. The most direct information is provided by the Sumero-Eblaite bilinguals, but most of them are still unpublished and in any case have to be used critically. The greatest part of our knowledge of Eblaite seems destined to come from the general archives, in which only a small proportion of the texts is spelled out in Eblaite with the rest being

Sumerograms and some Akkadograms. Thus the decipherment of Eblaite resembles that of cuneiform Hittite. In the latter, as we have seen, most of a tablet may consist of Sumerograms and Akkadograms with some Hittite words, or phonetic complements that may indicate Hittite suffixes spelled out phonetically. Since Hittite is Indo-European, the Hittite elements in a cuneiform Hittite text generally can not be confused with the Sumerian and Akkadian elements. But in this regard Eblaite is more difficult. For, though Sumerian is of a distinctive character, Akkadian and Eblaite are both Semitic so it is often hard to tell whether a Semitic word or inflectional element in an Ebla tablet is Eblaite or Akkadian.

The vocabulary, which embodies some inflection, leaves no doubt that Eblaite is Semitic. For example:

wa and *u*[11] "and" (as in all the Semitic languages)
ḫu-ta-mu is "signet ring" (as in Hebrew *ḫôtem-et*, and so forth)
se is "goblet" (compare *s^c* in Ugaritic)
ku₈-tim is "gold" (as in Hebrew *ketem*, Egyptian *k-t-m*, and probably Minoan *kidem-*)
qa-šu is "bow" (with feminine *-t*, Akkadian *qaštu*, Hebrew *qešet*, and so forth)
ši-ti is "beverage" (from the root *š-t-y* "to drink" in Hebrew, Akkadian, and so forth)
tam-mim is "perfect" (as in Hebrew and Arabic, and so forth)

Note that *ḫutamu* and *qašu* end in *-u*, the familiar nominative case ending, whereas *kutim* and *tammim* have no case ending. Furthermore, if the last consonant is weak (as in *sê* and *šitî*), the word is indeclinable and ends in a long

---

11. Both forms of this conjunction also occur in Hebrew, where, however, *wa-* can stand only in an originally closed syllable, or as an open syllable immediately before the accent. It becomes *û-* in a secondarily closed syllable or before a labial. Otherwise (that is, in open syllables not immediately before the accent) this conjunction becomes *w^e-*.

vowel that results from the coalescence of the weak consonant with the vowel that precedes it.

The pronouns bring out the Semitic character of Eblaite
quite clearly:

> *ana* is "I" (as in Aramaic and Arabic); the genitive *-ī* and the
> accusative *-nī* (common in Semitic)
> *anta* is "thou" (masculine) (as in Arabic, and so forth, and often
> with assimilation, *atta* as in Akkadian and Hebrew); the ac-
> cusative *kuwati* is "thee" (as in Akkadian)
> *šuwa* is "he" (Akkadian *šū*, compare Egyptian *sw*); the genitive
> is *-šu* (as in Akkadian); the accusative *šuwati* is "him" (as in
> Akkadian); and the genitive and accusative plural suffix *-šinu*
> is "their, them" (compare Akkadian *-šunu* and Egyptian *-sn*)

Since the Semitic identity of Eblaite cannot be (and has
not been) questioned, there is no point in belaboring the
obvious. Differences of opinion cluster about the classification of Eblaite within the Egypto-Semitic family of languages. Until many more of the Ebla tablets are published,
all of the proposed theories will continue to be premature.
Moreover, to a great extent the problem is chimerical as
long as the classification of Semitic (to say nothing of Egypto-Semitic) is in a state of flux. Indeed, it is too complex to
be settled in the foreseeable future.

As in Minoan, the lack of a uniform case system confronts us also in Eblaite. Some of the Semitic dialects
around the east Mediterranean in the Early and Middle
Bronze Ages had a variety of case inflections depending on
the particular word. Actually this is found even in Arabic,
though it is not the norm there. In Arabic (as in Akkadian)
most singular nouns are inflected with *-u* in the nominative, *-i* in the genitive, and *-a* in the accusative. Nouns with
these three case endings are called *triptotic*. Some nouns,
particularly proper names, have *-u* in the nominative but

the genitive and accusative fall together, ending in -*a*. Thus "Solomon" is *sulaymânu* in the nominative, but *sulaymâna* in the genitive-accusative. Such nouns with only two case endings in the singular are called *diptotic*. Other nouns end in -*a* regardless of the syntax; for example, *dunyā* "world" and *bušrā* "good news." Such nouns are called *indeclinable*. Eblaite and Minoan point to a high antiquity of different methods of case declension depending on the individual noun. Old Akkadian points to the equally ancient three-case system. It is futile to maintain that one system is "more original" than the other.[12]

The phonetics of Eblaite can help us understand problems in other groups of texts already discussed. For example in the Linear A and B syllabaries, *l* and *r* fall together. This phenomenon also characterizes the Egyptian hieroglyphs that do not differentiate *l* from *r*. Now at Ebla we find that *l* often takes the place of *r* (though never *r* for *l*). This puts the *l/r* phenomenon on a broader base.

An Eblaite treaty, "The So-called Treaty between Ebla and 'Ashur,' " has been republished.[13] Examination of a couple of its passages will illustrate the way in which Eblaite is being reconstructed.

1. kas$_4$-kas$_4$ /[14] du-du / 20 u$_4$ / tuš / ninda kaskal / kú / *an-da-ma*[15] /mí-du$_{11}$-ga / tuš / ninda-kaskal / ḫe-na-sum "The couriers are traveling; they have stayed twenty days; they have eaten their

12. If we do, we run into theory, the results of which will be acceptable only to those who share the same presuppositions. For example, if we stress, as a general linguistic principle, the widespread tendency toward analogic leveling, the variety of case systems would have been leveled out on the analogy of the triptotes.

13. Edmond Sollberger, "The So-called Treaty between Ebla and 'Ashur,' " *Studi Eblaiti* 3 (1980): 129–55.

14. I am following Sollberger's editorial devices in quoting his article. The slash indicates the end of a line. (The lines are quite short because the columns are narrow.) Semitic elements are italicized; Sumerian, is not.

15. The *da* sign represents also (as here) the syllable *ta*.

travel provisions. And you shall take care of their stay. Give them their travel provisions."

In this passage the only word in Eblaite is *an-da-ma (anta)* "thou" plus *-ma* "and." All the rest consists of Sumerograms to be pronounced in Eblaite translation. Accordingly, the interpretation depends mainly on our knowledge of Sumerian and very little on the Eblaite language of the text.

> 2. *su-ma / in* 10 nu-bànda / *ma-nu-ma / ás* / du-*tum* / 50 udu-udu / he-na-sum "If any among ten sergeants is on a journey, (they) shall give him fifty sheep."

The following analysis of words in this passage brings out the salient features of the Eblaite problem. Du-*tum* is the Akkadogram *aluktum* "journey." Du is Sumerian "to go" corresponding in meaning to Akkadian *alâku* "to go"; *alak tum* means a "going," thus a "journey." The word here, however, is to be read as the Eblaite equivalent. Since the case is genitive after the preposition *ás*, the Akkadian nominative suffix *-u* — in *-(t)u(m)*— is an indication that *alaktum* is not the Eblaite word but only the Akkadogram for it. There is some question as to whether *su-ma* "if" is Eblaite rather than an Akkadogram (that is, Akkadian *šumma* "if"). The prepositions *in* (here "among") and *ás* (here "on") and the generalized relative pronoun *ma-nu-ma* "whosoever" are Eblaite.[16]

The above examples suffice to show the orthographic nature of an Eblaite text, composed of Sumerograms and Akkadograms as well as Eblaite words spelled phonetically. It has been claimed that Eblaite is the first Semitic language

16. However, a case could be made for *in* and *ma-nu-ma* as Akkadian. Such doubts are the consequence of the Semitic character of both Akkadian and Eblaite. Since *ás* does not occur in Akkadian, it is definitely Eblaite.

to be written in cuneiform, antedating somewhat the earliest Akkadian texts ushered in by Sargon of Akkad. The presence of Akkadograms in the Ebla archives points in the opposite direction. Ebla in Syria followed the lead of Akkad both in using Sumerian script for writing Semitic texts and in establishing Sumero-Semitic bilingualism. The latter is not merely an abstract concept. It entailed an entire educational system and went hand in hand with a sophisticated, intellectual climate.

We cannot close the discussion of Ebla without facing the issue of "Ebla and Bible," which has given rise to so much acrimonious and foundationless controversy. Chronologically, attempts to place Abraham in the Ebla age are nonsensical. Abraham, according to any meaningful historical scheme, must be dated centuries after the Early Bronze archives of Ebla. For scholars who have no real sense of the scope and nature of the Bible, this terminates the discussion. However, once we realize the continuity of historic forces in the Near East, we discern that, at many levels, an early source can illuminate a much later source without any direct contact between them. The most demonstrable and specific evidence is linguistic, and the value of the following example of Eblaite-Hebraic equations is to be judged by the light that a specific Eblaite word sheds on an exceedingly strange form of the conjunction in Ruth 4:5.

It would seem probable that two thousand years of intensive biblical scholarship would have cleared up the difficulties in the Hebrew text. But some reflection on the vocabulary of biblical Hebrew will show why this is not so. There are about 8,000 different words in biblical Hebrew, and many of these words occur frequently. But about 1,700 of them occur only once. Determining the meaning of a word from a single context generally does not lead to convincing results. Ugaritic has clarified a number of Old Testament hapax legomena and Ebla is beginning to clear up others. The following Old Testament *crux interpretum* is an exotic combination of *û-* "and" plus the enclitic *-ma* "and." It may be described as a compound (and pleonastic) conjunction. *Û-* "and" is well known. But *-ma* (ubiquitous in Akkadian) was not recognized in Hebrew until the impact of Ugaritic in the 1930s.[17]

There is a passage in the Book of Ruth that has baffled commentators. Ruth was the widow of a Judean whose ancestral estate had to be redeemed from the party with a lien on it. This was in keeping with old Hebrew institutions.[18] In the normal course of events the redeemer would be the deceased's next of kin, who would also take the deceased's place as husband and sire a child in the name of the deceased. The goal was to preserve the line and estate of every house in Israel.

But another custom among the Northwest Semites complicates this. Sexual intercourse between two eligible people constituted marriage. In the rabbinic tractate, *Women,* there is a section, "Marriage," which states that any of three acts cements wedlock: to wit, (1) silver (for example, the payment of some *bonum* such as silver), (2) the writing of a marriage contract, or (3) sexual intercourse between the eligible man and woman.[19] It is interesting to note that the Northwest Semitic princess from Tyre and Sidon, Dido,

17. C. H. Gordon, *Ugarit Textbook* (Rome: Pontifical Biblical Institute, 1967), pp. 429–30 (§19.1402). A compound conjunction like *û + -ma* is the Latin *atque.*
18. Note Leviticus 25:25 (for redemption) and Deuteronomy 25:5–6 (for levirate marriage).
19. This section of the *Mishna* is called *Qiddûšîn* and starts: "The woman is acquired (as a wife) in (any of) three ways . . . she is acquired through *kesef* 'silver, money', through a *štar* 'written contract', and through *bî'a* 'sexual intercourse.'"

assumed that her love affair in the cave with Aeneas constituted marriage—an assumption that Aeneas, from a different background, did not share.[20] Therein lies the tragedy, that differences in background prevented two noble people from understanding each other. Fortunately, Ruth and Boaz shared the same Northwest Semitic background with the result that their story has a happy ending.

The Book of Ruth (3:7) says that she cuddled up at the feet of Boaz on a festive occasion after he had imbibed much wine. During the night he became aware of her presence and asked her to stay the night and to leave before dawn to avoid gossip (3:4). She had taken pains to look attractive for the occasion (3:1–6), after he had been noticing her with personal interest for some time (2:5–15; 3:10). Boaz promised to redeem the estate and marry her if he could eliminate the claim of the man who happened to be the next of kin (3:11–13). The latter, who did not know of the night Boaz and Ruth had spent together, was interested, in the marriage along with the redemption of the estate, for Ruth was a desirable young woman. Then comes the dramatic surprise (4:5). Boaz tells the next of kin to redeem the estate if he will but to realize that he (Boaz) has already acquired Ruth as wife. This changes the picture for the kinsman, not merely for emotional but also for economic reasons. The child to be born by Ruth will be the legal heir. Accordingly, the expense of redemption would do the next of kin no good economically, but to the contrary, it would impoverish his own family (4:6). Nor would it gain for him conjugal rights with Ruth, who already belonged to Boaz.

20. For a discussion of the affair in Vergil's *Aeneid*, see C. H. Gordon, "Vergil and the Bible World", *The Gratz College Anniversary Volume* (Philadelphia: Gratz College, 1971), pp. 111–30 and 114–15. Note particularly on p. 114, the contrast between Dido's assumption of marriage (*Aeneid* 4:316) and Aeneid's denial of any such thing (4:338).

Let us have a look at the text. "Boaz said: 'On the day you acquire the field from the hand of Naomi, (well and good); but I have acquired Ruth the Moabitess, the wife of the deceased, to raise the name of the deceased on his estate.' " A looser paraphrase would run thus. "If you insist on redeeming the estate and obtaining it from Naomi, you may do so. But you ought to know that I happen to have acquired Ruth as my wife for the purpose of siring an heir for the deceased on his estate."

The *crux interpretum* is the word *û-ma*,[21] which is to be rendered "but." This compound conjunction occurs so rarely, that it is still unknown to most specialists in Hebrew linguistics. This explanation of *w-m* in Ruth 4:5 occurred to me years ago but I forbore to publish it because the combination *û+ma* did not occur elsewhere. Eblaite *ûma* "and, but" appears repeatedly in the treaty cited above.[22] We do not infer that this is a borrowing or a survival from Eblaite into Hebrew. All we imply is that in Semitic, the enclitic *-ma* can be attached to the conjunction *û-*. The fact is that *w-m* in Ruth 4:5 remained intractable until it turned up at Ebla.[23]

21. Written consonantally *w-m* in the Hebrew texts. Vowels were supplied as diacritical marks centuries after the Hebrew text was composed and circulated as "The Scroll of Ruth."

22. Sollberger, "Ebla and 'Ashur,'" p. 155, lists (for this treaty text alone!) no less than five examples of *û-ma* "and, but" plus a context where it is used correlatively: *û-ma - - - û-ma* "and - - - and" in the sense of "either - - - or."

23. Our explanation is in strict keeping with the consonantal text of the Hebrew original without emendations or alterations of any kind.

Misunderstandings on the part of later generations led to imposing false vocalizations. Ordinarily, in other contexts, *wm't* is to be read *ûmê'et* "and from" and this is the way it has been vocalized here so that the meaning is distorted to "and from Ruth the Moabitess." Once this was done, the verb correctly written in our Hebrew text *qnyty* ("I have acquired") was mistakenly distorted into *qnyt* ("you have acquired") in total disregard of the final *-y*, so that the sense is changed to "and from Ruth the Moabitess you have acquired (that is, the field)." Actually the musical notation tells us (via a symbol called *'atnaḥ*) that the mid-verse division follows "from the hand of Naomi." The next word, *wm't* is *wm-* "but, and"

The ramifications of Eblaite are well illustrated by the Eblaite name *mu-nu-ti-um* (*mu-nu-ti* plus the nominative suffix *-um*) designating a town or region. This bears on the definition of Minoan *mi-nu-te* that occurs in Linear A lists of grains including *ku-ni-su* "emmer wheat" (HT 86:a5; 95:a2 and b2–3) or is followed by a grain determinative (HT 106:1).[24] The same word occurs in Ugaritic as *m-n-t* parallel to *k-s-m* "spelt (grain)." Note that "wheat of minnit" occurs as *ḥiṭṭê minnît* in Ezekiel 27:17. Mitchell Dahood has called attention to the Ebla-Ugarit-Hebrew correlation.[25] It is appropriate that this book on the *Forgotten Scripts* adds the Minoan *mi-nu-te* to the investigation of an Eblaite and Hebrew toponym.

---

plus *ʾēt*. The latter *(ʾēt)* is the untranslatable indicator of the definite, direct object (Ruth). (For a discussion of the difficulties in Ruth 4:5, see Jack M. Sasson, *Ruth* (Baltimore and London: Johns Hopkins University Press, 1979), pp. 119–36.

24. M. Dahood in his "Afterword" to Giovanni Pettinato's *Archives*, pp. 292–93.

25. The HT (Hagia Triada) tablets are cited according to the edition of W. C. Brice, *Inscriptions in the Minoan Linear Script of Class A* (Oxford and London: The Society of Antiquaries, 1961), plates I–XV.

9

A SAMPLING
OF UNLOCKED
TREASURES

As intriguing as the decipher-
ments may be, their importance lies more in what they
have opened up than in the ingenuity providing the keys.
Three thousand years of Egyptian and cuneiform writings
constitute a massive contribution to the story of civilized
mankind.[1]

1. The leading anthology has been edited by James B. Pritchard, *Ancient Near
Eastern Texts: Relating to the Old Testament,* 3d ed. with suppl. (Princeton: Princeton
University Press, 1969). There is a close interplay between literature and the

If we approach the subject statistically, we must conclude that the ancients were not primarily concerned with their own belles-lettres—what nation, ancient or modern, is? Like people all over, they were busied with survival, making a living, and holding on to their worldly goods. Vast assemblages of inscriptions like the Sumerian tablets of the Third Dynasty of Ur (c. 2000 B.C.) are economic. Dealing with cattle or grain, many of them by themselves seem trivial. But collectively they provide a detailed documentation of an entire economy that is hard to match throughout antiquity.

Babylonian mathematics and astronomy are of prime importance for the history of science. Yet the emphasis the Babylonians placed upon omens subordinated astronomy to the occult. The same happened with animal anatomy. The Babylonians were keen observers of the internal organs of sacrificial animals, but their observations were used for prognosticating the future. As a result, the Babylonians, who were real pioneers in the exact sciences, left a legacy of superstition and magic. The very word "Chaldeans," as the Babylonians were called, came to mean in Hebrew and in Greek "soothsayers" and "magicians." Thus what we see and appreciate in the ancients is not necessarily what they valued most in themselves. We are entitled to admire the Gilgamesh Epic more than the Ur III economic tablets, as long as we do not assume that our taste and values are universal.

The earliest literary writings tend to be poetry in which the gods play a prominent role. Such poetry often precedes literary prose. Sumero-Akkadian literature includes epic

visual arts. Cf. Pritchard's companion volume, *The Ancient Near East in Pictures: Relating to the Old Testament,* 2d ed. with supp. (Princeton: Princeton University Press, 1969).

and religious poetry before any real literary prose appears. Indeed, Greece illustrates the general situation rather well. The first known records in Greek are the dry, economic Linear B tablets; the first known literary masterpiece in Greek is Homeric epic. Prose literature in Greek comes later.

The unlocked written treasures of the Near East are vast. It has become futile to aspire to master the entire field. Even the subdivisions are too large for any one person to control. The age of the general cuneiformist is over. The scholar must decide not only whether he wants to specialize in Sumerian or Akkadian or Hittite or Ugaritic, but then also in which period or in what type of text. No incipient Egyptologist can expect to be knowledgeable in Old Egyptian, Middle Egyptian, New Egyptian, Late Egyptian, Ptolemaic-Roman Egyptian, Demotic, and Coptic. This state of affairs has, as a matter of fact, been creeping up for some time. (I know of two outstanding Coptologists of the first half of this century who never learned to read the hieroglyphs!)

Following are a few samples of the many categories of the deciphered literatures, and I shall try to convey an idea of the varieties of the texts and why they are of special interest.

The first four selections are Egyptian, the next six are cuneiform: Akkadian, Ugaritic, and Hittite. The Egyptian portions include a novelette, a love poem, wisdom literature, and an exotic "letter to the dead." The cuneiform passages embrace a historic annal, an administrative communication by an emperor to one of his satellites, a marriage contract reflecting distinctive customs, a royal *apologia*, an epic, and a ritual myth.

The first literary prose in the world developed, as far as

we know, during the Middle Kingdom in Egypt in the first centuries of the second millennium B.C. This literature takes the form of novelettes designed for pleasurable reading. Earlier, during the Old Kingdom, there were literary compositions such as the Pyramid Texts. But they are religious in character with the grim aim of perpetuating the posthumous lives of the pharaohs. The Middle Egyptian stories are secular and designed for sheer entertainment. All people, even illiterate tribesmen, narrate tales for each other's listening pleasure. But the Egyptians are the first on record to write stories purely for enjoyment with no serious concern or religious burden. Why the Egyptians, rather than the Sumerians, Hebrews, or Greeks?

Of all the nations of antiquity, the Egyptians most loved life in their sunny and fertile land. Though the Nile Valley was the closest approximation to Paradise on earth, the unpleasant accident of death befell mankind there just as everywhere else. But the Egyptian way of life was too good to end in a dreary Babylonian Irkalla, Hebrew Sheol, or Greek Hades. The Egyptian went to great lengths to preserve the body so that it could enjoy the same things after death as it had before. To a less cultivated people, the fiction of eating, drinking, playing, hunting, and fishing would suffice, but not to the Egyptians. For them an afterlife without entertaining reading matter just would not do. So they wrote down diverting tales and placed them in the tombs for the pleasure of the deceased. The cult of the dead also left records, ones that were not at all amusing and that dealt with the grim business of avoiding perdition and achieving salvation. For the Egyptians, too, faced a frightening judgment before achieving salvation. But in general the Egyptian thanatopsis was happy—as far as we know, everybody was saved (if one's record did not merit salvation, the cult of the dead provided the magic to turn the trick). On the west bank at Thebes the tombs of the nobles depict in lively colors the posthumous pleasures of harvesting fertile fields, playing games, boating with their families to catch fowl and fish along the banks of the Nile, and dining with entertainment provided by musicians and dancing girls. So many a diverting tale was left in the tombs to help cultivated ladies and gentlemen while away eternity.

The Middle Egyptian story of the shipwrecked sailor is an entertaining yarn of fanciful adventure, composed of tales within tales. A courtier has returned from a naval expedition to report to the pharaoh. Although the ship and crew have returned intact, the mission may have been unsuccessful. In any case the courtier is apprehensive about the effect his report may have on the pharaoh. A companion of the courtier tries to cheer him up by telling him about a successful report he once delivered to the pharaoh, and by reminding him that self-confidence and a ready tongue can extricate them from many a tight spot.

The companion's story constitutes the bulk of the text. He had been shipwrecked on a wondrous isle ruled by a huge serpent. He narrated his adventure to the serpent, who in turn told him its own life story. A rescue ship from Egypt brought the shipwrecked sailor, laden with gifts, back to the Nile Valley where he reported successfully to the pharaoh and lived happily ever after. He then admonishes the courtier to take heart from the happy ending. The courtier replies that to have survived an ordeal is not the same as facing one. A cheerful yarn is no more helpful to a man in deep trouble than giving water to a goose about to be slaughtered. Then the papyrus ends with a colophon that names and blesses the skillful scribe who copied the text carefully from beginning to end.

The Shipwrecked Sailor [2]

Said by a worthy companion: May your heart be whole, my prince! Lo, we have reached home. The mallet has been grasped, the mooring post driven in, and the prow rope placed on land. Praise is given, God is thanked. Everyone is hugging his colleague. Our crew has arrived safely, without loss of our personnel. We have reached the limits of Wawat, passed Senmut, come in safety, reached our land. Listen to me, my prince! I am devoid of exaggeration. Wash yourself. Put water on your fingers. You must answer when you are interrogated and speak to the king with self-assurance. You must answer without stammering. The mouth of a man can save him. His speech can gain him indulgence. You will act according to the dictates of your heart. It is frustrating to talk to you. But I shall tell you something like it that happened to me.

I had set out to the Sovereign's mines, gone down to the Great Green, in a ship one hundred and twenty cubits long and forty cubits wide. A crew of one hundred and twenty were on it, the pick of Egypt. They scanned the sky and scanned the land; their hearts were braver than lions. They could foretell a storm ere it came, a hurricane ere it happened. A storm broke while we were on the Great Green before we could reach land. The wind was lifted up. It redoubled with a wave eight cubits high. It struck off a plank for me. Then the ship died. Of those aboard it, not one survived. Then I was cast up on an island by a wave of the Great Green. I passed three days all by myself. My heart was my (only) companion. Lying in an arboreal shelter, I embraced the shade.

Then I stretched my legs to discover what I might put in my

2. The Egyptian text, in hieroglyphs, is edited by A. De Buck, *Egyptian Readingbook*, vol. 1. (Leiden: Nederlandsch Archaeologisch-Philologisch Instituut voor het Nabije-Oosten, 1948) pp. 100–06. The outstanding anthology of Egyptian literary texts is Miriam Lichtheim, *Ancient Egyptian Literature: A Book of Readings*, 3 vols. (*The Old and Middle Kingdoms; The New Kingdom; The Later Period*) (Berkeley and Los Angeles: University of California Press, 1973, 1976, 1980).

mouth. I found figs there, and grapes, all kinds of excellent vegetables, sycamore figs at all stages of ripeness, cucumbers as if cultivated, fish, and fowl; there was nothing lacking there. I proceeded to satiate myself and put some on the ground for there was too much for my arms. I cut a fire-drill, kindled a fire, and made a burnt offering to the gods.

Then I heard a thunderous noise. I fancied it was a wave of the Great Green. Trees were breaking, earth was quaking. Uncovering my face, I found it was a serpent coming, thirty cubits long. His beard was two cubits long. His body was plated with gold. His eyebrows were of real lapis lazuli. He coiled himself in front. He opened his mouth at me, while I was on my belly before him.

He said to me: Who brought you, who brought you, little one? Who brought you? If you delay in telling me who brought you to this island, I'll make you know yourself as ashes, made into something which cannot be seen.

I said: Though you speak to me, I am unable to hear it. Being in your presence, I do not know myself.

Then he put me in his mouth. He carried me to his pleasant lair. He set me down without harming me. I was whole, with nothing torn from me.

He opened his mouth, while I was on my belly before him. Then he said to me: Who brought you, who brought you, little one? Who brought you to this island of the Great Green, whose two sides are in the water?

Then I answered him, with my two arms bent in his presence. I said to him: I was going down to the mines on a mission of the sovereign in a ship one hundred and twenty cubits long and forty cubits wide. A crew of one hundred and twenty were on it, the pick of Egypt. They scanned the sky, scanned the land; their hearts were braver than lions. They could foretell a storm ere it came, a hurricane ere it happened. Every one was stouter of heart, and stronger of arm, than his fellow. There was not a misfit in their midst. A storm broke while we were on the Great Green, before we could reach land. The wind was lifted up. It redoubled with a wave eight cubits high. It struck off a plank for me. Then the ship died. As for those aboard it, not a one survived except me. Here I am by your side. I was brought to this island by a wave of the Great Green.

He said to me: Fear not, fear not, little one! Let not your face be pale! You have reached me. Behold! God has caused you to live and brought you to this Island of Ka. There is nothing which is not in it. It is full of every good thing. Behold you are going to spend month after month until you complete the fourth month in the midst of this island. A ship will come from home with a crew aboard whom you know. You will go home with them. You will die in your own city. How joyous it is to relate what one has experienced after the calamity has passed! I shall tell you something similar that happened on this island. I was on it with my siblings, and children were among them. We totaled seventy-five serpents, children and siblings, not to mention to you that other girl brought to me through a prayer.

Suddenly a star fell, and because of it, these went up in fire. It happened while I was not with them in the fire. I was not in their midst. I just about died for them when I found them in one pile of corpses.

If you are brave and control your heart, you will fill your embrace with your children, you will kiss your wife, you will see your house. Better is this than all else. You will reach home. You will be in it in the midst of your brethren.

Stretched out on my belly, I touched the ground before him. I said to him: I shall relate your power to the sovereign. I shall inform him of your greatness. I shall cause to be brought to you *ibi* and *ḥknw* oils, laudanum, and *ḫsyt* spice; temple incense wherewith any god is gratified. I shall tell what happened to me, what I saw of His (Excellency's) power. One will praise God for you in the city before the magistrates of the entire land. I shall slaughter for you bulls as a burnt offering, I shall sacrifice geese to you. I shall send you ships loaded with all the treasures of Egypt as is done for a god who loves people in a distant land, whom the people do not even know.

Then he laughed at me for the things I had said, which seemed foolish to him. He said to me: You are not rich in myrrh and all kinds of incense. But I am the ruler of Punt.

Myrrh is mine. That *ḥknw* oil you spoke of sending, it is the great product of this island.

When you have left this place, never again will you see this island which will have become water.

Then his ship came as he had foretold previously. I went and placed myself on a high tree. I recognized those aboard it. I then went to report it. I found he already knew it.

He said to me: Health, health, little one, homeward bound! You will see your children. Make my name fair in your city. Behold this is my request of you.

Then I fell on my belly with my arms bent in his presence. Then he gave me a cargo of myrrh, *ḥknw* oil, laudanum, *ḥsyt* spice, *tišpss* spice, perfume, mascara, giraffe tails, huge chunks of incense, elephant tusks, hounds, monkeys, baboons, and all fine luxuries. I loaded them on this ship. I placed myself on my belly to thank him.

He said to me: Behold you will reach home in two months. You will fill your embrace with your children. You will be rejuvenated at home. You will be buried (there).

Then I went down to the shore near the ship. I proceeded to call to the sailors on the ship. I offered praise on the shore to the lord of the island. Those aboard did likewise.

We sailed north to the residence of the sovereign. We reached the residence in two months. All was as he had said. I entered the presence of the sovereign. I gave him the gifts I had brought from the island. He praised God for me before all the magistrates of the land. I was made a courtier and endowed with serfs.

Look at me after I have reached land, after what I have seen and experienced! Listen to me! It is good for people to listen.

He said to me: Don't play the sage, my friend! Who gives water at dawn to a goose that one slaughters in the morning?

It is from its start to its finish as found in writing by the scribe with skilled fingers, Amony the son of Amon-ᶜa. May he live, prosper, and be hale!

The Egyptians believed that death did not end the responsibilities between the living and the dead. To the contrary, they felt that the deceased and their survivors continued to have practical obligations to each other. A widow should pour out water regularly to slake the thirst of her departed husband, while the latter owed his widow and children protection from enemies out to destroy their household. Misfortunes befalling the living constituted grounds for accusing the dead of not using their power to protect the family they had left behind. In that case the survivors of the deceased could write letters to the dead, exhorting them to action, or even threatening them with lawsuits. Such letters were placed in tombs, where it was thought that the living and dead have contact.

The following letter was delivered by a priest on behalf of a widow who refers to herself as "this handmaid" (the equivalent of "your humble servant"). The text is inscribed, spirally from the center toward the rim, inside a ceramic bowl. The figure of a woman is in the center. The widow has been showing consideration for her departed husband, whereas he has been doing nothing to ward off the malevolence of enemies who are out to destroy the household.

The Cairo Bowl [3]

(Given by Dedi, the priest of Antef, born of Iwnakht.)

As for this handmaid, Imiu, who is sick, you do not fight for her night and day with every man and every woman who is doing (harm) to her. Why do you want your gate to be desolated? Fight for her . . . so that her household may be established and that water may be poured out for you. If there is no (help) from you, then your house is destroyed. Can it be you do not know that this handmaid makes your house among

---

3. Alan H. Gardiner and Kurt Sethe, *Egyptian Letters to the Dead: Mainly from the Old and Middle Kingdoms* (London: Egypt Exploration Society, 1928), pp. 7–8, 22 and pls. VI, VIA.

men. Fight for [her]! Watch over her! Save her from all men
and women who are doing (harm) to her! Then will your house
and children be established. Good be your hearing!

Egypt produced a charming repertoire of lush love poetry. The following is the first of a collection of seven
poems, each with its "serial number" built into its start
and finish. This, being the first of the series, has "one" in
the initial and final lines. The "one" lady love, is compared to the lovely goddess Hathor whose epithet is "The
One."

A Heptad of Love Poems (Stanza 1)[4]

(Beginning of the sayings of the great happiness).
The one, sister without her rival
Comelier than all womankind.
Look, she is like the rising star
At the beginning of a lucky year.
She whose excellence shines, whose body glistens
When she glances her eyes are resplendent.
Sweet are her lip(s) when she speaks
Without a word in excess.
High, her neck; glistening, her nipple
Of true lapis lazuli, her hair.
Her arms, surpassing gold
Her fingers, like lotus lilies.
Plump of thigh, narrow of waist
Her legs reveal her beauty.
Her steps are graceful as she treads on the earth
She captivates my heart in her embrace.
She causes all the necks of men to turn to see her

4. Handsomely published in *The Library of A. Chester Beatty: Description of a
Hieratic Papyrus with a Mythological Story, Love-Songs, and other Miscellaneous Texts,*
by Alan H. Gardiner, F.B.A. *The Chester Beatty Papyri, No. I:* with thirty-seven
plates in monochrome and thirty in line by Emery Walker, Ltd., London: Oxford University Press and Emery Walker Ltd., 1931. See p. 30 and pls. XXII,
XXIIA.

Joyous is whoso embraces her
He is like the first of lovers.
When she goes forth abroad, one regards her
Like that other One.

Egyptian wisdom literature is addressed primarily to young scribes with a view to helping them get ahead in their profession. It can take the form of a father (himself an experienced scribe) instructing his son and admonishing him to cultivate virtues and to shun vices. The scribes were the élite upon whom the pharaoh's administration depended.

The Wisdom of Amenemope is the most polished example of Egyptian wisdom literature. It is carefully constructed in thirty chapters. Each chapter tends to be an essay on some particular virtue. Chapter XXVI below advises the reader not to be a social climber but to limit his camaraderie to his equals, to show respect to superiors, and to help the aged. The way singled out to assist the old is to give physical support to him when he is in his cups, exactly as one would to his own parent. In Ugaritic a model son is described as one who lends a hand to hold up a drunken father;[5] and an Old Testament prophet infers that a mother who cannot count on her children to take her by the hand and to lead her when she is inebriated, is indeed pathetic.[6] Chapter XXVI goes on to point out that kindness and affability are greater assets than the wealth of abrasive churls. The chapter ends with the affirmation that foresight averts catastrophe.

5. C. H. Gordon, *Ugaritic Textbook* (Rome: Pontifical Biblical Institute, 1967) text 2 Aqhat:II:19–20.
6. Isaiah 51:17–18.

The Wisdom of Amenemope[7]

Chapter XXVI.
Do not sit in the tavern
To hobnob with one greater than you;
Be he a youth, great through his position,
Or an elder by birth.
Be companionable with a man of your own station.
Re is helpful from afar.
If you see someone greater than yourself outside
Walk behind him respectfully.
Give a hand to the aged after he is inebriated with beer,
Respect him as his children would.
The arm is not hurt by being bared
The back is not broken by bending it.
A man, by speaking pleasantly, is not impoverished
(But gains) more than the riches of he who speaks abrasively.
The pilot who sees from afar
Does not let his ship capsize.

The final chapter of the *Wisdom of Amenemope* is the thirtieth. This clarified Proverbs 22:20 ("Have I not written for you Thirty"?), where "thirty" refers to an ideally structured book of wisdom. Chapter XXX recommends this wisdom book as enjoyable as well as beneficial, for it can transform the ignorant into an enlightened teacher. The final statement sums up the aim of wisdom literature: to train the able scribe for his promotion to the nobility.

---

7. This follows the edition of H. O. Lange, *Das Weisheitsbuch des Amenemope* (Copenhagen: Bianco Lunos Bogtrykkeri, 1928), chap. 26 on pp. 123–27; chap. 30 on pp. 134–36.

The Journal of the American Oriental Society 101 (no. 1) January–March 1981 is devoted to *Oriental Wisdom*, ed. by Jack Sasson. Particularly valuable is the chapter by R. J. Williams, "The Sages of Ancient Egypt in the Light of Recent Scholarship," pp. 1–19. A list of Amenemope papyri found since the publication of the long-known papyrus in the British Museum is on p. 2.

Chapter XXX.

Look at these thirty chapters!
They gladden, they instruct,
They are the foremost of all books,
They cause the ignorant to know.
If they are read in the presence of the ignorant,
He is made pure through them.
Be filled with them, put them in your heart,
And become a man for expounding them,
Being one who expounds through teaching.
If a scribe is skilled in his office,
He will find himself worthy of becoming a courtier.

The Old Testament provides a detailed account of Sennacherib's invasion of Judah in 701 B.C.[8] Hezekiah had tried to unite his neighbors against Assyrian domination and coerced the Philistine cities into accepting his leadership in the rebellion. His anti-Assyrian campaign was supported by the Egyptians who viewed the expansion of Assyria with alarm. Sennacherib invaded all of Hattu (Syria-Lebanon-Israel) and occupied all of Philistia and Judah except for Jerusalem. For the Jews, the salvation of Jerusalem meant that God had not forsaken his Holy City. For the Assyrians, Hezekiah was confined in Jerusalem "like a bird in a cage." Both accounts make it clear that Assyria had succeeded in reimposing its rule and tribute all over Hattu down to the Egyptian border.

Discrepancies between the Hebrew and the following Assyrian version have given rise to a view that they refer to different campaigns in the overlapping reigns of Hezekiah and Sennacherib. More likely, only one campaign is at issue, with the discrepancies attributable to expected differences in viewpoint and style. In the Hebrew account,

8. 2 Kings 18:13–19:37 and Isaiah 36:1–37:38.

Hezekiah offers to pay any tribute that Sennacherib may impose, on condition that the invading Assyrians depart to their own country. The Hebrew narrator, arranging the facts topically, spells out the nature and amount of the tribute before proceeding with the rest of the invasion and the withdrawal of the Assyrians. The Assyrian version, however, arranges the facts chronologically, with the Judeans delivering the tribute to Sennacherib in Nineveh after the Assyrian withdrawal. The Assyrian account happens to be more in keeping with the way we record history. In any case, common sense dictated that the tribute be paid after the siege of Jerusalem had been lifted and the Assyrian army had returned home. Paying before the withdrawal would have been sheer folly; and, though Hezekiah had been too bold in his schemes, he was anything but an impractical fool. The Hebrew and Assyrian accounts amplify each other so that the critical historian has the official version of both sides with which to work.

Sennacherib's Third Campaign[9]

In my third campaign I went to Hattu land. The fear of the splendor of my lordship overwhelmed Luli, King of Sidon, so that he fled afar in the midst of the sea and perished. Great Sidon and Little Sidon, Bet Zitti, Sarepta, Mahaliba, Ushu, Achzib, Acre, his strong-walled cities, where there were fodder and beverage, on which he depended—the terror of the weapons of my lord Assur overwhelmed them; they submitted at my feet. Tu-Baal I set on the throne over them. I imposed on him the payment of a permanent yearly tribute due my lordship.

As for Min(u)himu of the city of Samsimuruna, Sidonian Tu-Baal, Arvadite Abdi-Liti, Byblian Urumilki, Ashdodite

---

9. The cuneiform text is in Friedrich Delitzsch, *Assyrische Lesestücke*, 5th ed. (Leipzig: J. C. Hinrichs'sche Buchhandlung, 1912), pp. 65–68.

Mitinti, Budu-Ili of Beth-Ammon, Moabite Gambuzunatbi, Edomite Ayarammu—(yea) all the kings of Amurru brought sumptuous gifts, their heavy offerings fourfold to my presence and kissed my feet. But as for Sidqa, King of Ascalon, who had not submitted to my yoke, I deported and sent to Assyria the gods of his father's house, himself, his wife, his sons, his daughters, his brothers, the seed of his father's house. Sharruludari, son of Rukibti, their former king, I reestablished over the people of Ascalon and imposed on him the payment of tribute, of gifts to my royalty. He (now) pulls the straps (of my yoke).

In the progress of my expedition, I surrounded, captured, and plundered Beth-Dagon, Jaffa, Bney Braq, Azurru, the cities of Sidqa who did not submit to my feet quickly. The officials, princes, and people of Ekron who had thrown their king Padi, a sworn ally of Assyria, into iron chains and handed him over as an enemy to Hezekiah, the Judean, and he (Hezekiah) imprisoned him—their heart feared. They called on the kings of Egypt and the bowmen, chariotry, and cavalry of Ethiopia. A countless force had come to their aid. In the plain of Eltekeh their array was set against me and they readied their weapons. In the faith of my lord Assur, I fought with them and accomplished their overthrow. As for the Egyptian charioteers, and the charioteers of the King of Ethiopia, my hands captured them alive in the midst of the battle. Eltekeh and Timna I surrounded, captured, and plundered their booty.

I assaulted Ekron and killed the officials and princes who had perpetrated wrong. On staves around the city I hung their corpses. I reckoned as plunder the people of the city who had incurred guilt and shame. But as for the rest of them, who had not done wrong and shame, who had no guilt, I proclaimed their release. I caused their king, Padi, to go out from the midst of Jerusalem. I set him on the throne of lordship over them and imposed on him the tribute of my lordship.

But as for Hezekiah, the Judean, who had not submitted to my yoke, his forty-six strong-walled cities and the countless small towns in their vicinity, I besieged and captured by *(various operations and machines of war)*. Two hundred thousand and one hundred and fifty people, young and old, male and female;

horses, mules, asses, camels, herds (of oxen), flocks (of sheep and goats) without number I took out of their midst and reckoned as booty. I imprisoned him (Hezekiah) like a caged bird in the midst of Jerusalem, his royal city. I set up earthworks against him, and I turned back and hindered any trying to go out of his city gate. His cities, which I plundered, I detached from the midst of his land and gave to Mitinti King of Ashdod, Padi King of Ekron, and Ṣilli-Baal King of Gaza. Thus I diminished his land. I increased what their country had to pay above the former tribute, as gifts for my lordship, and I imposed it on them.

The fear of the splendor of my lordship overwhelmed Hezekiah. The irregulars and his crack troops whom he had caused to enter for strengthening Jerusalem his royal city, stopped fighting. With thirty talents of gold and eight hundred talents of silver *(and other assorted luxury items)*, his daughters, his palace women, male and female musicians, to the midst of Nineveh, the city of my lordship, after me he dispatched and sent a messenger for the paying of tribute and rendering of service.

Sennacherib's annals are transparently tendentious. The annalists who composed them were under general orders to praise the king and refrain from any criticism. The destruction he wrought and the booty he carried off are expressed in clichés and often exaggerated for his greater glory. Such annals, though devoid of objectivity, embody factual history that we can control from independent sources.

We are about to examine another type of royal text that is completely historical, without tendentiousness. It is a directive in the form of a Babylonian letter from the Hittite Emperor Hattusilis III to his vassal King Niqmepaᶜ of Ugarit. The purpose of the directive is to regulate the activities of the emperor's merchants of Ur(a) operating in Ugarit. Three issues are noteworthy: (1) their business interests were to be protected even to the extent that their debtors together with their families were to be enslaved if they could not pay what they owed the merchants; (2) The merchants were to remain in Ugarit seasonally but not throughout the year; and (3) they were not to acquire real estate in Ugarit, especially the king's buildings and lands. Genesis narrates that Abra(ha)m came from Ur of the Chaldees, which is not the Sumerian Ur, but the Ur near Harran in what is now south-central Turkey near the Syrian border. We know that Abraham and his descendants, Isaac and Jacob and the generations that immediately followed, engaged in trade, were kept on the move, and wanted to acquire real property in Canaan. For example, when the Prince of Shechem invited Jacob's family to join in an alliance, he tried to induce them by offering the same three items singled out by Hattusilis for his merchants of Ur(a): to wit, the right (1) to do business; (2) to settle permanently; and (3) to buy real estate.[10] Accordingly, Abraham of Ur at last fits into a documented historic movement: the settling of the merchants of Ur(a) in Canaan during the Late Bronze Age. How long the Ur(a) merchants had been operating in Canaan we do not know. It was their established *modus operandi* when Hattusilis wrote this letter in the thirteenth century B.C. It doubtless began before his reign and continued after it—how much before and after has not yet been determined. But if the directive does not tell us about the man Abraham, it provides information about the historic movement that brought him from Ur of the Chaldees to Canaan.[11] The following letter illustrates the raw material from which history is reconstructed.

10. Genesis 34:10, 21.
11. C. H. Gordon, "Abraham and the Merchants of Ura," *Journal of Near Eastern Studies* 17 (1958): 28–31; and C. H. Gordon, "Abraham of Ur" in *Hebrew and Semitic Studies*, the G. R. Driver Festschrift, (Oxford: Clarendon Press, 1963), pp. 77–84.

Hattusilis III and His Merchants of Ur(a)[12]

The seal of the Emperor, Hattusili, the Great King, King of Hittite Land.

To Niqmupa[c13] speak!

Thus have you said in my presence: "The Ur(a) merchants are very burdensome to the land of your vassal." So the Sun-god, the Great King, has established the following regulation for the people of Ur(a) with the people of Ugarit:

Let the men of Ur(a) ply their trade during the harvest in the midst of Ugarit, but in the days of winter they shall send (them) out of Ugarit to their (own) country. Yea, the people of Ur(a) in the winter shall not dwell in the midst of Ugarit nor shall they get real estate with their silver. And if (any) merchant of Ur(a) has caused the loss of silver of his tribute in the midst of Ugarit, the King of Ugarit shall not let him dwell in the midst of his land.

And if anyone cannot repay the silver of the people of Ur(a) lent to the people of Ugarit, the King of Ugarit shall deliver that man (the debtor) together with his wife and children into the hand(s) of the Ur(a) merchants.

And the merchants of Ur(a) shall not draw near the real estate of the King of Ugarit.

Lo, thus has the Sun-god, the Great King, established a regulation between the merchants of Ur(a) and the people of Ugarit.

The Nuzu tablets of the Amarna age were excavated in the 1920s and early 1930s near Kirkuk, Iraq. They provide us with the best documented account of life in any known community of antiquity. They cover four or five generations of several families in the fifteenth and fourteenth centuries B.C. The first Nuzu text translated below is a contract whereby a father named Nashwi adopts a man named Wullu, who is required to look after Nashwi for life.

---

12. Jean Nougayrol, *Le palais royal d'Ugarit IV* (Paris: Imprimerie Nationale, 1956), pp. 163–65.

13. Usually vocalized Niqmepa[c] with *e*. The spelling here with *-u-* is exceptional.

Tied in with the adoption is the wedding of Nashwi's daughter Nuhuya to Wullu. When this tablet was written, Nashwi had no son of his own, so that the adoption was to provide him with a line of heirs. However, Nashwi specifies that if a son of his own is born to him subsequently, that son, when dividing the estate with Wullu, is to take Nashwi's gods.

Possession of the household gods symbolized chief heirship with special reference to maintaining the family cult. The ancients felt that, in addition to the living and the dead, the family included the household gods. To prevent alienation of Nashwi's real property, Wullu is not to marry another woman. Thus Wullu's children must be born of Nashwi's daughter Nuhuya. If Wullu weds another woman, he forfeits all claim to Nashwi's real property.

When the man joins his wife's family rather than vice versa, Assyriologists call the union "*erêbu*-marriage." In such unions the position of the woman is higher than that of her husband. He enters this type of matrimony for economic gains, but in exchange he subordinates his family ties to hers. If he fails to do so, he is, so to speak, disowned and disinherited.

A Nuzu Contract of Adoption and Marriage[14]

The adoption tablet of Nashwi son of Arshenni.
He adopted Wullu son of Puhishenni. As long as Nashwi lives, Wullu shall give (him) food and clothing. When Nashwi dies, Wullu shall inherit.

Should Nashwi beget a son, (the latter) shall divide equally with Wullu but (only) Nashwi's son shall take Nashwi's gods. But if there is no son of Nashwi's, then Wullu shall take Nashwi's gods. And (Nashwi) has given his daughter Nuhuya

14. Text 51 in C. J. Gadd, "Tablets from Kirkuk," *Revue d'Assyriologie* 23 (1926): 49–161; see especially 126–27, 155.

as wife to Wullu. And if Wullu takes another wife, he forfeits Nashwi's land and buildings. Whoever breaks the contract shall pay one mina of silver (and) one mina of gold.

The Nuzu tablets include a dossier of interest for the history of government and law. Kushiharbe,[15] the mayor of Nuzu, and his henchmen (notably Peshkillishu, Kibiya, and Ziliptilla) had been committing crimes against citizens and their property. As today, corrupt officials were not surprising in antiquity. But this dossier is noteworthy in showing that people could unite against the top municipal official and in court put so much incriminating testimony on record that at least impeachment must have ensued.

The following offenses are excerpted from the dossier in the order that the tablets have been published. (1) The mayor robbed a storehouse and returned what he took only after the victim paid him off. (2) The mayor's gardener filched a citizen's fertilizer. When the victim dared to complain, he was intimidated by threats of flogging and of property damage. (3) The mayor denied he had illicit intercourse with a certain woman. Unfortunately for the mayor, another witness testified that he had procured that same woman for the mayor on another occasion. (4) Soldiers testified that one of the mayor's gangsters took a large number of sheep for the central government. However, he never delivered them to the government or returned them. (5) One of the mayor's ruffians was accused of adulterating milk with water. (6) The mayor filched roofing material from a woman trying to maintain her own house. (7) One of the mayor's gangsters seized a citizen's sheep, which in his own house he cooked and ate. (8) Another one of the

15. Also written Hushiharbe, with ḫu- as the first syllable. The name is not Hurrian, but Kassite. The Kassite Dynasty was then ruling Babylonia.

ruffians agreed to pay for a sheep, which he then took but would not pay for. (9) A woman paid one of the gangsters with a sheep to attend to a lawsuit for her. He took the sheep and rendered no service. When she inquired about her sheep, he beat her, kept the sheep, imprisoned her, and extorted a sizeable quantity of copper, stating that this sum was for settling old accounts. (10) Another citizen complains that the same gangster pocketed a fee but then did not attend to the lawsuit he had been paid for. (11) Another citizen voices a similar charge. (12) This time the gangster not only took sheep but seized a young woman and held her captive in his house for eleven months. (13) The same rascal tore the door off a vacant house and proceeded to strip the place.

The People versus the Mayor[16]

1. So declares Ninuari: "Kushiharbe robbed me from my own storehouse. Two shekels of gold, one ox, and two rams I paid to Kushiharbe; then he restored to me (what he had stolen)."

2. So declares Mar-Ishtar: "The manure for one and a half homers of land, the gardener of Kushiharbe took away from me, so I said: 'Why do you take away my manure?' and he replied: 'As for you, he has ordered you to be beaten and your district he has ordered to be devasted.' I was scared and took off."

3. So declares Ziliptilla: "Last year Mrs. Bizatum made Mrs. Humerelli stay with her. Shimitilla and I went over at night, we summoned her and brought her to the place of Kushiharbe, and he had intercourse with her." Kushiharbe replied: "No! Absolutely not! I did not have intercourse with her!" So declares Palteya: "I called Humerelli and took her over to the trysting house of Tilunnaya and Kushiharbe had intercourse with her." Kushiharbe replied: "I swear that Palteya did not bring Humerelli to the trysting house of Tilunnaya, nor did I have intercourse with her!"

16. See tablets 1–14 in R. H. Pfeiffer and E. A. Speiser, "One Hundred New Selected Nuzi Texts," *Annual of the American Schools of Oriental Research* 16 (1935–36): 13–20, 65–75.

4. Thus the soldiers of Nuzu declare: "Ninety-two sheep Kibiya received. Neither did he take them to the palace nor yet did he return them to us."

5. Shukriteshub declares (to Kibiya): "And why indeed do you bring your milk to be diluted with water?"

6. Thus declares Hanatum: "I was roofing my house and spreading reed matting over the beams. Ziliptilla and a slave of Kushiharbe came over and stripped the house of all the matting. Kushiharbe took away the reed mats."

7. Thus declares Dubbiya: "One male sheep Ziliptilla took away, cooked it in his house, and ate it."

8. Thus declares Shukriteshub: "One sheep Peshkillishu took for a price, but the price he did not pay."

9. Thus declares Hinzuri the wife of Ziliya: "I gave to Peshkillishu a sheep as a fee and thus I said: 'With regard to my lands, attend to my lawsuit with Kariru.' My lawsuit he did not conduct. I spoke about my sheep, so he smote me and kept my sheep. Furthermore he seized me and took six minas of copper. Thus he said: 'For last year I am taking (this).' "

10. Thus declares Hatarte: "I was journeying to Hanigalbat and on account of my lawsuit they handed me over to Peshkillishu. One sheep, one bowl of bronze, and two doors Ahummisha paid as a fee to Peshkillishu but he did not attend to my lawsuit."

11. Thus declares Haziri: "Six shekels of refined silver I gave to Peshkillishu and thus I said: 'Give (them) to Kushiharbe and let him attend to my lawsuit.' One chariot ornament I gave (in addition). But he did not attend to my lawsuit. Peshkillishu kept the six shekels of silver and the chariot ornament."

12. Thus declares Shutrama: "Peshkillishu took away and kept two of my sheep. My bride he took away and for eleven months imprisoned her in his house."

13. Thus declares Arshawa: "I happen to reside in Tursha. Peshkillishu entered my house, tore off the door, took it, and stripped the house."

Ugarit has yielded the most important literary discovery that has been unlocked since the decipherment of Egyptian and Mesopotamian cuneiform. Among the epics from Ugarit, *The Legend of King Kret* is especially significant in bridging early Greek and Hebrew literature. The affinities are best illustrated by its "Helen of Troy" motif: a king's uniquely destined wife must be retrieved by her spouse from another king's domain. Thus King Menelaus must recover Helen from Troy. Kret must win his bride Hurrai from King Pibol's walled city of Udum. And Abraham must retake Sarah, first from Pharaoh and later from Abimelech, King of Gerar to found their royal line.[17] There are three epic literatures rooted in the Late Bronze Age around the shores of the East Mediterranean: Greek, Ugaritic, and Hebrew. All three are royal with the Helen of Troy motif. The connection between Homer and the Bible was not perceived until Ugarit emerged as the connecting link.

The following selections from *The Legend of King Kret* deal with: (1) Kret's refusal to accept Pibol's bribe to depart from Udum and give up the quest for Hurrai's hand in marriage; (2) El's blessing at the wedding of Kret and Hurrai; (3) Latpan's (El's) exorcizing the demon of disease from Kret; and (4) Kret being told to abdicate because, on account of his illness, he has been failing to fulfil the social obligations of kings.

From the Legend of King Kret [18]

1. What need have I for silver
   And yellow gold together with its place
And eternal slaves
   Teams of three horses

---

17. Genesis 17:6, 16.
18. The Epic of Kret is translated and annotated by C. H. Gordon, "Poetic Legends and Myths from Ugarit," *Berytus* 25 (1977): 34–59. Where the restorations are certain (for example, from repetitions of the same passages), they are not enclosed in brackets.

Chariots from the yard of a handmaid's son?
But what is not in my house shalt thou give!
Give me Lady Hurrai
The fine of family
Thy firstborn
Whose charm is like Anath's charm
Whose loveliness is like Astarte's loveliness
Whose brows are gems of lapis lazuli
Eyes, bowls of alabaster
Whom El has given in my dream
In my vision, the Father of Man
To bear a family to Kret
Yea a lad to the servant of El!

2. A cup El takes in his hand
A goblet in the right
He verily blesses
El bless the generous Kret
Strengthens the Good One, Lad of El:
"The wife thou takest, O Kret,
The wife thou takest to thy house
The girl thou causest to enter thy court
Will bear thee seven sons
And an eighth (daughter), Octavia;
To thee she will bear the lad Yasib
One who suckles the milk of Asherah
Who sucks the breasts of the Virgin Anath
The wet nurses of the Good and Fair Gods."

3. Latpan, God of Mercy, declares:
"Who among the gods will drive out the disease
Exorcizing the illness?"
None among the gods answer him.
A second, a third time, he says:
"Who among the gods will drive out the disease
Exorcizing the illness?"
None among the gods answer him.
A fourth, a fifth time, he says:
"Who among the gods will drive out the disease

Exorcizing the illness?"
None among the gods answers him.
A sixth, a seventh time, he says:
"Who among the gods will drive out the disease
Exorcizing the illness?"
None among the gods answers him.
And Laṭpan, God of Mercy, declares:
"Return, my sons, to your seats
Yea to the thrones of your excellencies!
I shall perform magic
Verily to stay the hand of the disease
Yea exorcizing the illness."

4. Thou hast let thy hands fall into evil case
Thou dost not judge the case of the widow
Nor adjudicate the cause of the broken in spirit
Nor drive away those who oppress the poor.
Before thee thou dost not feed the fatherless
Nor behind thy back the widow.
For thou art a brother of the bed of sickness
Yea a companion of the bed of disease.
Step down from the kingship that I may rule
From the sovereignty that I may be enthroned thereon!

Text 52 of the Ugaritic corpus embodies in dramatic form a myth associated with the fertility cult.[19] This tablet was recited (or, more exactly, sung) with a ritual designed to usher in a sabbatical cycle of good years. (1) The opening selection below portrays the spirit of privation that must be banished. (2) Later the god El dallies with two women. On his virility depends the character of the new cycle of seven years. It is the all-important alternative of fertility or famine. He succeeds in impregnating them. (3) Then, climactically, El impregnates the women again so that they

19. To what extent this was acted out before the devotees is hard to determine. But the explicit sex in the libretto explains why the Hebrew moralists reacted against the Canaanite fertility cult and branded paganism as "whoring" after other gods.

bear the Seven Good Gods who usher in a prosperous sabbatical cycle. The poem ends on the happy note of abundance.

From The Birth of the Seven Good Gods[20]

1. Death-and-Evil[21] sits.
In his hand is the staff of privation
In his other hand, the staff of bereavement.
They prune him with the prunings of the vine
They switch him with the switchings of the vine
And he is felled in his fields like a vine.

2. Lo, one (woman) will go down
Lo, the other will rise
Lo, one will cry "Father, Father!"
Lo, the other will cry "Mother, Mother!"
Let El's hand be long like the sea
Yea El's hand like the flood!
El's hand became long like the sea
Yea El's hand like the flood.
El takes two effigies
Two effigies from the top of the fire
He takes and puts (them) in his house.
As for El, his rod is low
    As for El, the staff of his hand hangs down.
He lifts (his bow) and shoots heavenward
    He shoots a bird in the heavens
    He cleans and sets it on the coals.
El tests the two women.
If the women will shout
"O husband, husband!
Thy rod has fallen
Lowered is the staff of thy hand!"
While the bird roasts on the fire
Broils on the coals,
Then the two women are wives of El
Wives of El and his forever.

20. Translated and annotated by Gordon, "Poetic Legends," pp. 59–64.
21. A compound name like Amon-Re or Yahweh-Elohim.

But if the women shout
"O Father, Father!
Thy rod has fallen
Lowered is the staff of thy hand!"
While the bird roasts on the fire
Broils on the coals,
Then the two girls are daughters of El
Daughters of El and his forever.
And lo the two women shout
"O husband, husband!
Thy rod has fallen
Lowered is the staff of thy hand!"
While the bird roasts on the fire
Even broils on the coals.
So the women are wives of El
Wives of El and his forever.
He bends
Kisses their lips
Lo their lips are sweet
Sweet as grapes.
From kissing there is conception
From embracing there is impregnation
They go into travail
So that they bear
Dawn
And Dusk.
Word is brought to El:
"The wives of El have borne!
What have they borne?"
"My two children
Dawn and Dusk!"

3. He bends, their lips he kisses
Lo their lips are sweet.
From kissing there is conception
From embracing there is impregnation.
He sits, counts to five
The assembly
The twain go into travail

And they bear
They bear the Good Gods
The Islanders, Sons of the Sea
Who suck the nipple of the breast.
Word is brought to El:
"My two wives, O El, have borne!
What have they borne?"
"The Good Gods
The Islanders, Sons of the Sea
Who suck from the nipple of the breast."
They put a lip to earth
A lip to heaven
And there enter their mouth
The birds of heaven
And fish from the sea
And there proceed piece by piece
They set both right and left in their mouth
But they are not satisfied.
"O wives I have wed
O sons I have begotten!
Get on with making preparations
In the midst of the Wilderness of Kadesh!
There you will be sojourners
Of the stones
And of the trees
Seven complete years
Yea eight cycles
Until the Good Gods walk the field
Roam the corners of the steppe."
And they met the Guard of the Sown:
"O Guard, Guard, open!"
And he opened an aperture for them
So that they entered.
"If [there is b]read, give that we may eat!
If there is [wine] give that we may drink!"
And the Guard of the Sown answered them:
"There is bread to eat
There is wine. . . . "

The Apology of Hattusilis III is a text of unusual political, psychological, and religious interest. Hattusilis seized power and became emperor even though according to Hittite law he was not the heir to the throne. His older brother Muwattallis legitimately succeeded their father Mursilis. Later, Muwattallis died without leaving a legitimate son so that an illegitimate one, Urhiteshub, with the help of Hattusilis, was enthroned in accordance with the official rules of succession. Meanwhile, Hattusilis functioned as a regional king within the empire.

Urhiteshub regarded his able uncle Hattusilis with misgivings and tried to reduce his military and territorial power. Thus Hattusilis composed his Apology to show that Urhiteshub was the offender and that Hattusilis in self-defense had to depose him and take his place.

All of life, including politics and war, went hand in hand with a convenient theology among the nations of the ancient Near East. We have noted how Sennacherib invaded Judah in accordance with the command of his god Assur, while Hezekiah resisted in accordance with his reliance on Yahweh. Hattusilis did what he did in keeping with the will of his goddess Ishtar. He had entered into a covenant with the goddess who promised prosperity and sovereignty to both him and his successors as long as they would revere her as their special deity. (This motif is called a "covenant" by theologians.) Hattusilis's relationship to Ishtar is like Abraham's to Yahweh. In both cases a deity grants sovereignty to a man of the kingly class[22] in exchange for dynastic devotion.

David of Judah, who supplanted Saul of Benjamin of

---

22. For God's covenant with Abraham as the founder of the royal line, see Genesis 17:6.

Israel, required an Apology to legitimize his usurpation of the throne. For David, like Hattusilis, succeeded to the throne by his own initiative and ability, not by the laws of succession. David is accordingly portrayed as wronged by Saul[23] much like Hattusilis by Urhiteshub.

An unusual feature of the Apology is the goddess's relationship with the queen and Ishtar's granting the royal pair the greatest of blessings: love between husband and wife.

The Apology of Hattusilis[24]

1. So says King Hattusilis, the Great King, King of Hattu, son of Mursilis, the Great King, King of Hattu, grandson of Shuppiluliuma, the Great King, King of Hattu, descendant of Hattusilis, King of Kussaras.

2. I declare Ishtar's power. Let mankind hear it! And in the future, among the gods of My Majesty, of his son, of his grandson, of the seed of My Majesty, let there be reverence to Ishtar.

3. My father Mursilis begot us four children: Halpasulupis, Muwattallis, Hattusilis and a daughter DINGIR-MEŠ-IR-is.[25] I was the last child of them all. And while I was still a child and a groom, my Lady Ishtar, through a dream, sent my brother Muwattallis to my father Mursilis (saying): "For Hattusilis, the years are few; he is not to live. Now give him to me and let him be my priest. Then he will live." And my father took me, a child, and gave me as a servant to the goddess. Serving as a priest to the goddess, I poured libations. At the hand of Ishtar, my Lady, I saw prosperity. Ishtar, my Lady, took me by the hand and guided me.

4. When, however, my father Mursilis became a god (died), and my brother Muwattallis sat on the throne of his father, I

23. 1 Samuel 24:15–23.
24. Published by Edgar H. Sturtevant and George Bechtel, *A Hittite Chrestomathy* (Philadelphia: Linguistic Society of America and University of Pennsylvania, 1935), pp. 42–83. The numbers of the sections reflect lines drawn across the tablet by the scribe to indicate the parts into which he divided the text.
25. Her name is written with three Sumerograms followed by the Hittite case ending. All this tells us about the sound of her name is that in the nominative, it ended in *-is*.

became, in the presence of my brother, general of an army, and then my brother appointed me to the post of chief of the Meshedi and gave me the Upper Country to rule. So I ruled the Upper Country. Before me, Armadattas son of Zidas had been ruling it.[26] Now because Ishtar my Lady favored me, and my brother Muwatallis was well disposed toward me, when people saw my Lady Ishtar's favor toward me (and) my brother's kindness, they envied me. Armadattas son of Zidas and other people began to stir up hostility against me. They brought malice against me and I had misfortune. My brother Muwattallis named me for the wheel.[27] But my Lady Ishtar appeared to me in a dream, and in the dream said this to me: "Shall I abandon you to a (hostile) god? Do not fear!" And I was cleared from the (hostile) god. Since the goddess, my Lady, held me by the hand, she never abandoned me to the hostile god, (or) the hostile court, and the weapon of an enemy never overthrew me. Ishtar my Lady always rescued me. If sickness ever befell me, even while ill I beheld the power of the goddess. The goddess, my Lady, always held me by the hand. Because I was an obedient man and because I walked before the gods obediently, I never pursued the evil course of the sons of mankind. You, O goddess my Lady, always keep rescuing me. Has it not been (so)? The goddess my Lady never passed me by at any(?) time. To an enemy she never abandoned me, nor to my envious opponents in court did she ever abandon me. If there was any plot of an enemy, any plot of a litigant (or) any plot of the palace, Ishtar my Lady always held protection over me; she always rescued me. Ishtar my Lady delivered my envious foes into my hand and I completely destroyed them.

5. When my brother Muwattallis came to understand the situation and there remained no evil thing against me, he took me back and placed in my hand the infantry and chariotry of Hattu land so that I commanded all the infantry and chariotry of Hattu land. My brother Muwattallis kept sending me (on expeditions). Since Ishtar my Lady granted me favor, wher-

26. Armadattas's loss of power to Hattusilis explains the cause of the subsequent enmity between them.
27. Perhaps some kind of ordeal.

ever I turned my eyes to the country of an enemy, no enemy turned his eyes back on me. I kept conquering the countries of the enemy. The favor of Ishtar my Lady was mine. Whatever enemy there was in the lands of Hattu, him I drove out of the lands of Hattu. But whatever countries of the enemy I conquered while I was a youth, that I shall make into a tablet separately and set before the goddess.

6. When my brother Muwattallis, by the word of his god, went down into the Lower Country and left Hattusas, my brother took the gods of Hattu and the *manes* and carried them down into the Lower Country. Afterwards all the country of the Gasga, the land of Pishurus, the land of Ishupitta (and) the land of Daistipassa revolted and took away the land of La———, the land of Maristas and the walled cities; and the enemy crossed the Halys River. . . .[28] Then during the years my brother Muwattallis was in the land of Hattu, the country of all the Gasga made war and devastated the land of Sadduppa (and) the land of Dankuwa. Now my brother Muwattallis sent me (into battle) and established (my headquarters) in Pattiyarigas. But he gave me troops and chariotry in small numbers. Then I took along auxiliary troops and chariotry in small numbers and marched. I cut off the enemy in the city of Hahhas and gave him battle. Now Ishtar my Lady marched before me, and I defeated him and set up a memorial stela.[29] Every Hittite whom he had brought thither, I took away and resettled (in his original place), and I took (his) allies and delivered them to my brother. This was my first manly deed. Ishtar my Lady in this campaign, for the first time called my name.[30]

7. The foe of the city-state of Pishuru came and invaded, and the city-states of Karahnas and Maristas were in the midst of the enemy. On that side the city-state of Takkastas was his boun-

---

28. An untranslatable passage.

29. The text has the Sumerogram šu "hand." In Hebrew *yād* "hand" can mean a "memorial" monument, including a memorial stela of victory (1 Chronicles 18:3). Unless it can be shown that this meaning of šu occurs in Sumerian, we are apparently dealing with a meaning of "hand" current in the West (that is, "Greater Hattu," which embraces Canaan as well as Anatolia).

30. The same expression occurs in Isaiah 45:3, 4, where Yahweh calls Cyrus by name, thus proclaiming his divinely designated kingship.

ary, and on this side the city-state of Talmaliyas was his boundary. (His) horses were eight hundred teams, and as for his infantry there was no counting. My brother Muwattallis sent me (against him) but gave me (only) one hundred and twenty teams of horses but of infantry not a single man was with me. But now, just as Ishtar my Lady marched before me, just so I conquered the enemy by my own resources. Now when I had slain every man who was an ally (of the foe), the enemy fled. The various cities of Hattu land which had been cut off were now taking up arms and began to attack the enemy. I set up a commemorative stela in Wistawanda. And even as the favor of Ishtar my Lady was with me, so the weapon I held I enclosed and set it up before the goddess my Lady.

8. (An account of further successes)

9. When once my brother had come (and) marched into the land of Egypt, the countries that I had resettled . . . I led into the field the army and chariotry of this country for my brother in the land of Egypt. And now because, in the presence of my brother, the army and chariotry of Hattu land were in my hand, I commanded them. Now when Armadattas, son of Zidas, saw the kindness of Ishtar my Lady and of my brother toward me, he did not show any reverence, but he together with his wife and children tried to bewitch me, and he filled Samuhas, the city of the goddess, with witchcraft. But when from the land of Egypt I was going back, I went to Luwazantiyas to pour libations for the goddess and worshipped the goddess. At the command of the goddess I married Puduhepa the daughter of Bentisharri the priest. We fulfilled (the oracle to marry) and the goddess gave us the love of husband and wife. And we got sons and daughters. Then the goddess, my Lady, [said] to me: "With (your) house be subject to me!" Then I together with my house put my trust in the goddess. And for us the goddess dwelt within the house we were making. . . .[31] Hakpissas revol[ted] and I drove out the men of Gasga and subjected them. So I became king of the land of Hakpissas and you became queen of Hakpissas.

---

31. An untranslatable passage.

10. When, however, from the palace an indictment was brought again, Ishtar my Lady at that time showed her power and afterwards produced a new indictment. They found witchcraft against Armadattas together with his wife (and) children and established it against him, for he filled Samuhas, the city of the goddess, with witchcraft. The goddess, my Lady, made him lose the case to me and my brother handed him over to me together with his wife, children (and) house. Then my brother said to me: "Sippa-LÚ-is is not in (it)." Because my brother made me win against him in court, I did not later pay back malice. Because Armadattas was a [related(?)] man, and besides was old and was [si]ck, I let him off (and) I let Sippa-LÚ-is [off]. When I had let them off and did nothing to them, I indeed sent [Armadattas] and his son to Alashiya.³² I took half his lands and gave it back to Armadattas. . . .³³ My brother died and I out of respect for my brother di[d noth]ing (selfish), but because my brother had no [legitimate] son, I took Urhi-Teshub, the son of a concubine, and made him lord in the land of Hattu. I put the whole army in his hand. He was for the lands of Hattu the great king and I was king in Hakpissas. With army and chariotry I marched. Since Nerikkas had been in ruins from the day of Hantilis, I took and rebuilt it. The countries which bordered Nerikkas and made Neras and Hassuras their boundary, I subjected all of them and made them tributaries. . . .³⁴

11. Now when Urhi-Teshub thus observed the benevolence toward me, he envied me and brought trouble on me. He took away from me all my subjects and also Samuhas he took way from me. As for the waste lands I had resettled, all these also he took away from me and weakened me. But Hakpissas, on account of the word of a god, he did not take away from me. Because I was a priest of the storm god of Nerikkas, he did not take it away from me. Out of respect for my brother, I did not act recklessly. I submitted into the seventh year, but through the word of a god and the suggestion of a man, he tried to

32. Generally thought to be Cyprus.
33. An untranslatable passage.
34. An untranslatable passage.

destroy me, and took Hakpissas and Nerikkas away from me.
Now, however, I no longer submitted and I made war against
him. But when I made war against him, I did not do it as a
crime. Did I rebel against him in the chariot or rebel against
him in the palace? As an (honorable and open) enemy I declared (war) against him (thus): "You started hostilities against
me. Now you are a great king; but, as for me, the one fortress
which you have left to me, of (that) fortress I am king. Come!
Ishtar of Samuhas and the storm god of Nerikkas shall decide
the case for us!" Now whereas I wrote thus to Urhi-Teshub,
if anyone says: "Why did you formerly set him on the throne,
and why are you now declaring war against him?" (I can answer: "That would have been well and good) if he had never
started hostilities against me." Would (the gods) have subjected
an upright great king to a little king? But because he started
hostilities against me, the gods subjected him to me in this case.
When I communicated to him these words (saying) "Come
on!" to him, he marched out from Marassantiyas and came to
the Upper Land. Sippa-LÚ-is, son of Armadattas, was with
him and he appointed him to muster the troops of the Upper
Land. But because Sippa-LÚ-is was hostile to me, he did not
succeed against me.

12.   While Ishtar my Lady had been previously promising me
the kingship, at that time Ishtar my Lady appeared to my wife
in a dream (saying): "Before your husband I shall march, and
all of Hattusas shall be led by your husband. Because I have
thought highly of him, I never abandoned him in a lawsuit or
to any god. So I shall elevate him and appoint him to the
priesthood of the sun goddess of Arinnas. So you too, make me,
Ishtar, your patron goddess." Ishtar my Lady stood behind me.
What she told me, happened. Then Ishtar my Lady demonstrated power abundantly. Ishtar my Lady appeared in dreams
to whatever nobles Urhi-Teshub had banished (saying): "You
are urged to your strength, for I, Ishtar, have turned back all
the lands of Hattu to Hattusilis." Then also I saw the power
of Ishtar abundantly. Though at no other time had she abandoned Urhi-Teshub, she now locked him up like a pig in a pen.
But as for me, the Gasga men who had been hostile, supported

me, and all Hattusas supported me. Out of respect for my brother, I did not act rashly. Into Samuhas to Urhi-Teshub I marched back and brought him down like a captive. I gave him several walled cities in Nuhasse and he dwelt there. Another scheme he plotted and would have driven off to Babylon, but when I heard the matter, I caught him and banished him across the sea. They sent Sippa-LÚ-is across the border, so I confiscated his house and gave it to Ishtar my Lady and Ishtar my Lady thereafter granted me (my desires) step by step.

13.   Now I was the son of a king, and became the chief of the Meshedi. I, chief of the Meshedi, became king of Hakpissas. I, King of Hakpissas, then became the Great King. Thereupon Ishtar my Lady delivered into my hand my enviers, foes, and opponents at law. Some died by the weapon, some died on the (fated) day, and I got rid of them all. Ishtar my Lady gave me the kingship of the land of Hattu and I became the Great King. My Lady Ishtar took me as a prince, and placed me into kingship. Those who had been well disposed toward the kings before me became well disposed toward me. They began to send me messengers and began to send me gifts. But such gifts as they kept sending, they had not sent to any of my fathers and forefathers. Whatever king owed me homage, paid me homage. But (the lands) that were hostile to me, I conquered. I added district after district to the lands of Hattu. Those who had been hostile to my fathers and forefathers, made peace with me. Because the goddess, my Lady, had thus favored me, I, out of respect for my brother, did not act rashly. I took my brother's son KAL-as and set him a throne there in Dattasas, the place that my brother, Muwattallis, had used for (his) place. . . .[35]

14.   (Curse against any who alienate any descendant of Hattusilis and Puduhepa from devotion to Ishtar)

15.   In the future whatever son, grandson, or future descendant of Hattusilis (and) Puduhepa shall ascend (the throne), let him be reverent to Ishtar of Samuhas among the gods.

---

35. An untranslatable passage.

BIBLIOGRAPHY

Barber, F. J. W. *Archaeological Decipherment: A Handbook.* Princeton University Press, 1974.

Bauer, Hans. *Das Alphabet von Ras Schamra.* Halle/Salle: Max Niemeyer Verlag, 1932.

————*Entzifferung der Keilschrifttafeln von Ras Schamra.* Halle/Salle: Max Niemeyer Verlag, 1932.

Bermant, Chaim, and Weitzman, Michael. *Ebla: A Revelation in Archaeology.* New York: Times Books, 1979.

Brice, W. C. *Inscriptions in the Minoan Linear Script of Class A.* Oxford and London: The Societies of Antiquaries, 1961.

Buck, A. De. *Egyptian Readingbook.* Vol. 1. Leiden: Nederlandsch Archaeologisch-Philologisch Instituut voor het Nabij-Oosten, 1948.

Bibliography

Budge, E. A. Wallis. *The Decrees of Memphis and Canopus.* 3 vols. London: Kegan Paul, Trench, Trubner, 1904.

————. *The Rosetta Stone,* 1913. Reprinted. London: British Museum, 1927.

————. *Rise and Progress of Assyriology.* London: Martin Hopkinson & Co., 1925.

Bush, Frederick William. *A Grammar of the Hurrian Language.* Ann Arbor, Michigan: University Microfilms, 1965.

Camp, L. Sprague de. *The Ancient Engineers.* Norwalk, Connecticut: Burndy Library, 1966.

Ceram, C. W. *Hands on the Past.* New York: Alfred A. Knopf, 1966.

Cleator, P. E. *Lost Languages.* New York: John Day, 1959.

Corré, Alan D. "Anatomy of a Decipherment." *Wisconsin Academy of Sciences, Arts and Letters* 55 (1966):11–20.

Cowley, Arthur E. *Aramaic Papyri of the Fifth Century B.C.* London: Oxford University Press, 1923.

Delitzsch, Friedrich. *Babel and Bible: Two Lectures on the Significance of Assyriological Research for Religion.* Chicago: Open Court Publishing Company, 1903.

————. *Assyrische Lesestücke.* 5th ed. Leipzig: J. C. Hinrichs'sche Buchhandlung, 1912.

Deuel, Leo. *The Treasures of Time.* Cleveland: World Publishing Company, 1961.

Dhorme, Edouard. "Le déchiffrement des tablettes de Ras Schamra." Reprinted in *Recueil Edouard Dhorme,* Edited by Edouard Dhorme. Paris: Imprimerie Nationale, 1951.

Doblhofer, Ernst. *Voices in Stone.* New York: Viking Press, 1961.

Donner, H., and Röllig, W. *Kanaanäische und aramäische Inschriften.* Vol. 1. Wiesbaden: Harrassowitz, 1962.

Drioton, E., and Vandier, J. *L'Egypte.* 4th ed. Paris: Presses Universitaires de France, 1962.

Driver, G. R. *Semitic Writing: From Pictograph to Alphabet.* New rev. ed. London: Oxford University Press, 1976.

Falkenstein, Adam. *Grammatik der Sprache Gudeas von Lagas.* 2 vols. Rome: Pontifical Biblical Institute, 1949, 1950.

Frankfort, Henri. *The Birth of Civilization in the Near East.* New York: Doubleday (Anchor), 1956.

Friedrich, Johannes. *Hethitisches Elementarbuch.* 2 vols. Heidelberg: Carl Winter, 1940–46.

————. *Hethitisches Wörterbuch.* Heidelberg: Carl Winter, 1952 (3 suppls. 1957, 1961, 1966).

————. *Extinct Languages.* New York: Philosophical Library, 1957.

————. *Die hethitischen Gesetze,* Leiden: Brill, 1959.

————. *Hethitisches Keilschrift-Lesebuch.* Heidelberg: Carl Winter, 1960.

————. *Entzifferung verschlossener Schriften und Sprachen.* 2d ed. Heidelberg: Springer-Verlag, 1966.

Gadd, Cyril J. "Tablets from Kirkuk." *Revue d'Assyriologie* 23 (1926):49–161.

Gardiner, Allan H. *The Library of A. Chester Beatty: Description of a Hieratic Papyrus with a Mythological Story, Love-Songs, and other Miscellaneous Texts. The Chester Beatty Papyri, No. 1,* London: (Oxford University Press and Emery Walker Ltd.), 1931.

————. *Egyptian Grammar,* 3d ed. New York: Oxford University Press, 1957.

————, and Sethe, Kurt. *Egyptian Letters to the Dead: Mainly from the Old and Middle Kingdoms.* London: Egypt Exploration Society, 1928.

Gelb, I. J. *A Study of Writing.* Rev. ed. Chicago: University of Chicago Press, 1963.

Godley, A. D., ed. and trans. *Herodotus*. Vols. 1 and 2. Cambridge, Mass.: Harvard University Press (The Loeb Classical Library), 1957.

Gordon, Cyrus H. "Western Asiatic Seals in the Walters Art Gallery." *Iraq* 6 (1939):3–34 (pls. II–XV).

———. "Abraham and the Merchants of Ura." *Journal of Near Eastern Studies* 17 (1958):28–31.

———. "Abraham of Ur." In *Hebrew and Semitic Studies*, edited by D. W. Thomas, and W. D. McHardy (The G. R. Driver Festschrift). Oxford: Clarendon Press, 1963.

———. *The Ancient Near East*. New York: Norton, 1965.

———. *The Common Background of Greek and Hebrew Civilizations*. New York: Norton, 1965.

———. *Evidence for the Minoan Language*. Ventnor, N.J.: Ventnor Publishers, 1966.

———. *Ugarit and Minoan Crete*. New York: Norton, 1966, 1967.

———. *Ugaritic Textbook*. Rome: Pontifical Biblical Institute, 1967.

———. "*Ki-de-ma-wi-na* (HT 31:4)." *Kadmos* 8 (1969):131–33.

———. "Greek and Eteocretan Unilinguals from Praisos and Dreros." *Berytus* 19 (1970):95–98.

———. "Vergil and the Bible World." *The Gratz College Anniversary Volume*. Philadelphia: Gratz College, 1971.

———. "The Decipherment of Minoan and Eteocretan." *Journal of the Royal Asiatic Society* (1975):148–58.

———. "Further Notes on the Hagia Triada Tablet No. 31." *Kadmos* 15 (1976):28–30.

———. "Poetic Legends and Myths from Ugarit." *Berytus* 25 (1977):5–133.

Güterbock, Hans G., and Hoffner, Harry A. *The Hittite Dictionary of the University of Chicago*. Vol. 3, fasc. 1, 1980.

Hammond, N. G. L. *A History of Greece to 322 B.C.* 2d ed. Oxford: Clarendon Press, 1967.

Kahn, David. *The Codebreakers*. New York: Macmillan, 1967.

Kaster, Joseph. *Wings of the Falcon: Life and Thought of Ancient Egypt*. New York: Holt, Rinehart & Winston, 1968.

Kent, Roland G. *Old Persian: Grammar, Texts, Lexicon*. 2d ed. New Haven: American Oriental Society, 1953.

Knudtzon, J. A. *Die El-Amarna Tafeln*. Leipzig: Vorderasiatische Bibliothek, 1907–15.

Lange, H. O. *Das Weisheitsbuch des Amenemope*. Copenhagen: Bianco Lunos Bogtrykkeri, 1928.

Lichtheim, Miriam. *Ancient Egyptian Literature: A Book of Readings*. 3 vols. Berkeley and Los Angeles: University California Press, 1973, 1976, 1980.

Marblestone, Howard J. "Dictys Cretensis: A Study of the Ephemeris Belli Troiani as a Cretan Pseudepigraphon." Ph.D. dissertation, Brandeis University, 1970 (distr. by University Microfilms, Ann Arbor, Michigan).

Marinatos, Spyridon. "Grammátōn didaskália." *Minoica* (Festschrift for Johannes Sundwall), Berlin: Akademie-Verlag (1958): 226–31 (pl. I).

Matthiae, Paolo. *Ebla: An Empire Rediscovered*. Garden City, N.Y.: Doubleday, 1981.

Mercer, S. A. B. *The Tell el-Amarna Tablets*. 2 vols. Toronto: Macmillan, 1939.

Meriggi, Piero. *Grammatica*. In *Manuale di Eteo Geroglifico*, vol. 1. Rome: Edizioni dell'-Ateneo, 1966.

———. *Testi*. In *Manuale di Eteo Geroglifico*, vol. 2. Rome: Edizioni dell'-Ateneo, 1967.

Meyer, Eduard. *Geschichte des Altertums*, 4 vols. 2d ed. Stuttgart and Berlin: Gotta'sche Buchhandlung, 1907–39.

Nougayrol, Jean. *Le palais royal d'Ugarit IV.* Paris: Imprimerie Nationale, 1956.
Pettinato, Giovanni. *Catalogo dei Testi Cuneiformi de Tell Mardikh—Ebla.* Naples: Istituto Universitario Orientale di Napoli, 1979.
———. *Testi Amministrativi della Biblioteca L. 2769.* Naples: Istituto Universitario Orientali di Napoli, 1980.
———. *The Archives of Ebla.* Garden City, N.Y.: Doubleday, 1981.
Pfeiffer, R. H., and Speiser, E. A. "One Hundred New Selected Nuzi Texts." *Annual of the American Schools of Oriental Research* 16 (1935–36): 9–168.
Platon, N., and Brice, W. C. *Inscribed Tablets and Pithos in Linear A System from Zakro.* Athens: Library of the Archaeological Society, 1975.
Poebel, Arno. *Grundzüge der sumerischen Grammatik.* Rostock: privately printed by the author, 1923.
Pope, Maurice. *The Story of Decipherment: From Egyptian Hieroglyphic to Linear B.* London: Thames & Hudson Ltd., 1975.
Pritchard, James B. *Ancient Near Eastern Texts: Relating to the Old Testament.* 3d ed. with suppl. Princeton: Princeton University Press, 1969.
———. *The Ancient Near East in Pictures: Relating to the Old Testament,* 2d ed. with suppl. Princeton: Princeton University Press, 1969.
Richard, Roberta J. "HT 31—An Interpretation." *Kadmos* 13 (1974):6–8.
Saggs, H. W. F. *The Greatness That was Babylon.* New York: Hawthorn Books, 1962.
Salonen, Armas. *Die Hausgeräte der alten Mesopotamien II: Gefässe.* Helsinki: Finnish Academy of Sciences, 1966.
Sasson, Jack M. *Ruth.* Baltimore and London: Johns Hopkins University Press, 1979.
Soden, W. von. *Grundriss der Akkadischen Grammatik.* Rome: Pontifical Biblical Institute, 1952 (2d rev. ed. with suppl., 1969).
Sollberger, Edmond. "The So-called Treaty between Ebla and 'Ashur'." *Studi Eblaiti* 3 (1980):129–55.
Stieglitz, Robert R. "The Eteocretan Inscription from Psychro," *Kadmos* 15 (1976): 84–86.
Sturtevant, E. H., and Bechtel, G. *A Hittite Chrestomathy.* Philadelphia: Linguistic Society of America and the University of Pennsylvania, 1935.
Thureau-Dangin, François. *Die sumerischen und akkadischen Inschriften.* Leipzig: Hinrichs, 1907.
Ungnad, Arthur. *Grammatik des Akkadischen,* rev. by L. Matouš. Munich: Beck, 1964.
Virolleaud, Charles. "Les inscriptions cunéiformes de Ras Shamra." *Syria* 10 (1929): 304–10 (pls. LXI–LXXX).
———. "Le déchiffrement des tablettes alphabétiques de Ras-Shamra." *Syria* 12 (1931):15–23.

INDEX